Spices and Herbs

Akeel Graham

What exactly is meal planning? Simply put, it is planning all of yours or your family's meals for the week. Some simple planning ahead can make life a little easier and healthier, and we are all about that! (1, 2) If you have never attempted meal planning and the idea sounds overwhelming, don't stress! This article is focused on meal planning for beginners. We'll first discuss the benefits, and then we will dive into the steps.

Or if you just want to start meal planning now, check out our simple and delicious Whole Life Meal Plan!

Meal Planning Benefits
- Saves money: When you meal plan for the week, your grocery trips will become more focused, and your cart will be filled with foods that you planned to buy instead of foods that you picked up on impulse. Meal planning can also help limit the number of times that you get food delivered or dine out; cooking at home is usually a less expensive option. (3)
- Saves time: At first, meal planning might feel more time-consuming, but we promise that once you get in the habit, it will become much faster and easier. Planning your meals ahead of time will also help reduce the time you spend thinking about and coming up with meals during the week. Plus, this can help cut back on your grocery store trips – a huge timesaver too!
- Provides more variety: When you sit down and think about what you want to purchase or cook in advance,

this will help you vary the cuisine, flavors, and recipes.

- Creates less stress: Wouldn't it be great to not worry about what you're going to make for breakfast, lunch, and dinner every day? Meal planning takes the guesswork away and gives you a plan for what to cook for the week.
- Ensures healthier eating: When you plan your meals, you are in better control of the ingredients you put in your body. Although you don't have to cook every meal to be healthy, meal planning does provide great motivation to get back to the kitchen. At To Taste, we believe cooking is one of the best ways to take control of your health!
- Prevents food waste: Meal planning promotes conscientious grocery shopping and helps you pay better attention to a food's shelf life. When you plan ahead and stick to a list, you are less likely to buy extra foods that may go bad.

10 Steps for Meal Planning Success
Now that you know the benefits, let's review the points to consider when meal planning. Follow these 10 steps to make meal planning a snap!

1. Decide your meal planning style.
   Meal planning looks different for different people.

   Some people plan the meals they are going to cook and eat for the week and use that to make a grocery list.

Other people cook and portion out all of their meals for the week using meal prep containers, so that limited cooking, if any, is done throughout the week.

And for others, it is a combination of the two!

Choose the meal planning style that works best for you! Remember that the whole idea is to plan your meals for the week; you can prep or not prep as much as you want in advance.

2. Stock up on pantry and fridge staples.

Keeping your pantry and fridge stocked with basic ingredients helps make meal planning easier and less intimidating.

As described in our Healthy Pantry Staples and Fridge Essentials article, this guarantees healthy eating and cooking at home. If you are starting off with limited ingredients, the initial investment might seem large. However, once you have these basic ingredients, recipe selection and grocery list development will be much easier!

3. Equip your kitchen.

Set yourself up for success! It is hard to cook and store meals if you don't have the necessary equipment. Proper kitchen equipment includes everything from knives and pans to storage bags and storage containers.

4. Schedule a planning and shopping day.

    I usually do both my planning and shopping on Sunday due to time constraints, but I definitely find it easier to plan on Saturday and shop on Sunday. Figure out whichever day works best for you! Try to keep these days consistent, as this will determine the days and meals that you plan.

    Of course, there will be times that you will need to shop or plan on a different day, but staying consistent can help make meal planning part of your weekly routine.

5. Evaluate your week, then plan meals accordingly.

    Once you have the basic tools, staple ingredients, and a scheduled planning/shopping day, it's time to actually start meal planning!

    Think about the week ahead – early meetings that require grab-and-go breakfasts, a Friday lunch out with co-workers, evening soccer practice with your kids, etc. Any event or situation that will alter your time or ability to cook should be noted. A late evening out might indicate a need for a crockpot or no-cook meal.

6. Decide which meals you want to cook.

    Don't want to decide the meals yourself? We've already done the work for you! Simply download our Whole Life Meal Plan for FREE, or purchase the Premium version for step-by-step recipe videos, nutrition tidbits, and a pre-made grocery list!

Remember, meal planning looks different for different people. Decide how many meals you want to cook per week, how many meals you will eat out, and which meals you will rely on convenience foods. This will all be dependent on your schedule and lifestyle; you do not have to cook every meal!

A lot of people choose to focus their energy on dinner. Dinner leftovers also make great lunches.

You might have to prepare several lunches depending on your household. Do you pack your kid's lunch? Do you take lunch to work? Sandwiches, wraps, salads, and grain bowls packed with fresh fruit and veggies are all easy lunch options.

Breakfasts and snacks can also be simple. Whole grain toast with peanut butter and fresh fruit requires little planning and is a nutritious start to your morning. If you want to make your own breakfast items, consider making them in bulk and freezing. Muffins, pancakes, and energy bites can all be frozen and defrosted overnight.

Snacks don't usually require much preparation; consider fresh fruit, nuts, yogurt, cheese, vegetables, and hummus. If you want to prepare your own snacks, trail mix and granola are easy recipes that last for weeks.

7. Select your recipes.

It's always a good idea to take note of any refrigerated or frozen ingredients that you have on hand before looking at recipes, especially if they have a limited shelf life. Once you have an idea of which ingredients you want to include in your meal plan, then start looking for recipes.

Don't forget about side dishes! Roasted vegetables and salads are some of our favorite quick and easy sides.

Select recipes that you can cook in the time you have available. These can be traditional recipes that you follow or your own ideas based on your ability to cook without a recipe. Rely on household favorites that you already cook frequently, then consider adding a new recipe or new variation once or twice a week. Vary flavors, cuisine types, and proteins.

Check out our base recipes for ideas on how to take one recipe and vary it in unlimited ways.

Multi-functional recipes can help make meal planning simpler. For example, a black bean corn salad can be used in a quesadilla one day, tossed with greens the next, and then served as a burrito bowl with whole grains and veggies the next!

Try to think in advance for future meals. Pizza on Monday? Make extra marinara sauce and freeze it in portions. Taco Tuesday? Make extra beans and freeze. Making extra food can be helpful for a future dinner or lunch. Speaking of Pizza Monday and Taco Tuesday, some people find it easier to follow theme days like these – one less thing to think about!

Rely on your crock pot or Instant Pot for evenings when you won't have a lot of time to cook.

Finally, remember that there is no rule that says you can't eat the same meal multiple times in one week!

8. Make your grocery list and shop.

List all of the ingredients you will need to prepare the meals you planned for the week. Then, put them in order to match the layout of the grocery store. This might sound crazy, but we promise that it saves time!

Next, decide which ingredients and recipes you want to spend time preparing. Do you want to cut a whole head of cauliflower, or do florets sound more appealing? Do you want to cook a whole chicken, or would buying a rotisserie chicken free up some time to cook something else?

Although you already took an inventory of the ingredients you have on hand, it's not a bad idea to return to the pantry or fridge to double check that you didn't list something you already have before heading to the store.

Once at the grocery store, stick to the list, but remain flexible. Take advantage of sales and specials that can help lower your grocery bill! Use our Ingredient Guide to choose the best ingredients.

9. Prep on Sunday (or whatever day you choose).
This step is definitely optional, but we are guessing that you have a pretty busy life since you are reading an article on meal planning and could benefit from some advance prep!

You can decide how much time you want to commit based on what makes sense for you and your family. Meal prep Sunday can be as basic as chopping vegetables, measuring spices, or washing and portioning fruits for packed lunches.

I like to use Sundays to prepare breakfast foods, snacks, sauces, and large batches of beans. As mentioned before, some people like to fully prepare their meals for the week, and that's great! Just be sure to consider shelf life. Not all foods can maintain their quality for a full week.

We'd love for you to join us each month to meal prep some nourishing recipes to your taste in our LIVE cooking classes!

10. Follow your plan, but remain flexible.
Obviously you want to stick to your plan after all of that hard work, but there are going to be days when

unpredictable events arise or you don't have the energy to make what you originally planned. That's okay; just have a back up plan! Master some go-to pantry staple recipes, such as baked tostadas or Instant Pot curry, and learn basic culinary techniques (such as those found in our online knife skills 101 course) so you can whip up a meal quickly without a recipe if needed.

Table of contents

1.The Magic of Spices and Herbs........................ **1**

What's in a Spice (or Herb)?

The Global Kitchen

Need-to-Know Spices and Herbs

2.The Spices... **22**

Allspice

Asafetida

Caraway

Cardamom

Cayenne / Red Pepper Flakes

Cinnamon

Cloves

Coriander

Cumin

Curry Leaves

Fenugreek

Ginger

Juniper Berry

Mace

Mustard

Nutmeg

Paprika

Pepper

Poppy

Saffron

Salt

Sesame

Star Anise / Anise Seed

Sumac
Turmeric
Vanilla

3.The Herbs **195**
Arugula
Basil
Bay Leaf
Borage
Chives
Cilantro
Dill
Fennel
Garlic
Green Onion
Horseradish
Lavender
Lemongrass
Marigold
Mint
Oregano / Marjoram
Parsley
Rosemary
Sage
Savory
Scented Geranium
Tarragon
Thyme
Watercress

4.The Blends **357**
Berbere
Cajun Spice

Curry Powder / Garam Masala
Five-Spice Powder
Harissa
Herbes de Provence
Khmeli Suneli
Mole Poblano
Seven-Spice Powder / Shichimi Togarashi
Za'atar

Understanding the magical world of spices is a little like unlocking a door to the power of your senses. This chapter will help familiarize you with the aromas, colors, and flavor characteristics of spices and herbs, providing you with sufficient confidence to begin transforming drab dishes into evocative works of flavor art—all without recipes. We'll illuminate the distinctions between spices and herbs, explain how to design and fortify a spice rack that caters to your cooking needs, and help you solve the riddles of the mysterious flavors of regional cuisines. You'll learn tips on how to best store your spices and herbs, and even how to grow your own herbs at home.

What's in a Spice (or Herb)?

Currently, many chefs use the words *spices* and *herbs* interchangeably when discussing flavoring agents for food, but historically, these terms have referred to different parts of the plant. To make the best use of them in your kitchen, it's helpful to understand the precise distinction. Both spices and herbs are derived from plants. When a plant is used purely for medicinal purposes, the entire plant is called an herb. In the culinary context, however, *herbs* refers solely to the leafy portion of the plant, either dried or fresh, while *spices* indicates the seeds, berries, twigs, roots, bark, or flower of the plant (usually dried). Some plants are considered to be both spices and herbs, such as an oregano leaf and oregano seed. The flavor of an oregano leaf, however, is quite distinct from that of its seed, which will break down or bloom in flavor according to how you cook it.

UNDERSTANDING SPICES

A spice is usually the more pungent, concentrated, and flavorful form of the plant, and is derived from a plant's root, seed, bark, flower, or fruit. Turmeric and ginger, for example, are root spices, while cumin, mustard, and nutmeg are seeds. The inner layer of bark from the cassia tree in Indonesia provides most of the world with cinnamon, and saffron comes from the flower of the saffron crocus, originally grown in India and Greece.

During the Middle Ages in Europe, a cargo of spices from Indonesia (referred to as the Spice Islands at the time), was literally worth its weight in gold, ounce for ounce. Among the upper classes, spices like cinnamon, cloves, nutmeg, and pepper were all in vogue. They were highly cherished for two reasons: they helped preserve food, and they could camouflage the flavor of slightly rotting food. In the sweltering climate of India, cooks had already been using pepper to prevent food from spoiling, since the second century BCE.

The antimicrobial oils originally produced by a plant to prevent animals and other organisms from eating it are what gives a spice its characteristic aroma. Since our tongue is only capable of tasting a limited variety of flavors—sweet, salty, sour, and bitter—spices add more complex fragrances. In a sense, spices might be considered perfume for food.

Though European cooks have been playing with the spices grown in tropical climates since people began making voyages to procure them—adding nutmeg to cream sauces, for example—most of the spices sourced from the hot climates of the Middle East and Asia have characteristic associations with the foods that come from those climates: spicy (hence the word *spice*), nutty, sweet, and hot, ranging from the mildly zesty flavor of coriander seed to the walloping blaze of a hot pepper.

UNDERSTANDING HERBS

Herbs are the tender, leafy parts of the plants that usually thrive in the more temperate growing climates of the United States and Europe. When settlers first came to America, they found parsley, anise, pennyroyal, sorrel, wild leeks, and lavender growing wild. In Europe, herbs had been used for ritualistic, ceremonial, and medicinal purposes for longer than spices, and their cuisines reflect this.

Think of the flavors of comfort food: poultry stocks simmering with bay leaf, tomato sauces with oregano and basil, Russian borscht with fresh dill, soothing teas like lemon balm and mint, potatoes roasting with rosemary and chives, and Thanksgiving turkey stuffed with sage. Herbs can be mixed into cheeses and cream sauces, tucked under the skin of roasting chicken, or sprigged onto fish. Unlike spices, herbs are most flavorful when used fresh.

Although some herbs, like arugula and mustard greens, can be spicy, in general, herbs tend toward flavors that are bitter, astringent, tart, or savory rather than sweet or fiery. While spices are earthy, nutty, warm, and reminiscent of fall, herbs can be as refreshing and zingy as spring. The aroma of chopped fresh cilantro can transform any kitchen with its garden fragrance, and a sprig of thyme or basil can add a punch of vibrant green to any dish.

Since herbs are native to temperate climates, they can be grown at home and used fresh. You can use homegrown biennial herbs, such as oregano, marjoram, lavender, sage, and thyme, year-round. You might even have your own rosemary bush or bay laurel tree in your backyard and supply your whole neighborhood with rosemary and bay leaves. When cooking with spices and herbs, a rule of thumb—at least until you are ready to experiment with more adventurous flavor blends—is to combine spices with spices and herbs with herbs.

The Global Kitchen
When cinnamon, mace, pepper, nutmeg, and cloves could be procured only through a dangerous two-year journey, such spices were understandably cost prohibitive to anyone other than the elite. Today, on the other hand, diverse spices from all over the world can be purchased at your local grocery or spice store, or even online. The case is somewhat similar with the use of herbs.

Until recently, however, the only fresh herb most people consumed was often that lone sprig of parsley decorating their plate —and most people didn't even eat that. Perhaps they had some dried oregano and basil in their pantry, or a curry blend to add to a tuna casserole, but the use and understanding of spices and herbs was limited. Now that has drastically changed; people are creating entire salads out of fresh herbs, layering them into casseroles, grinding and mixing their own spice blends, and growing their own herb gardens on their windowsills. Cooking with spices and herbs need no longer be a mystery, or even particularly difficult.

With so many people discovering the joys and health benefits of these complex flavors, why are salt and pepper still the only flavoring agents on the table? Actually, the historical reason goes back to seventeenth-century France, when it was decided that sugar should be served at the *end* of the meal, rather than used interchangeably with salt. It was also determined that pepper was the only flavor that could be added to cooked food without changing the dish's essential character.

Nevertheless, why not have a cumin shaker on the table, too, as they did in ancient Greece or do in modern-day Morocco, or at least include cumin in your spice rack? Today's kitchen has the potential to become enticingly multicultural. But with so many spices and herbs available, figuring how to put them to use can be challenging. This guide can help you decide which spices are most critical to your personal spice rack and set you on your way to creating your own global kitchen.

SPICES AND HERBS BY CUISINE

When experimenting with international and regional cuisines, it's important to keep in mind that spices and herbs aren't the only flavoring agents available, and in some cultures, spices are used less than other seasonings. In Russia, for example, pickle juice might be used as a flavoring for salads, and in Korea, meat might be marinated in fish sauce. Finding the right balance of spices and foods native to those cultures is the secret. Is there a specific regional cuisine you find yourself cooking the most, or is there a cuisine with which you'd like to experiment? Consider organizing your spice rack according to some of the following groupings:

CAJUN
bay leaf, cayenne pepper, oregano, paprika, rosemary, thyme

CARIBBEAN
allspice, cinnamon, cloves, ginger, nutmeg

CHINESE
citrus peel, cloves, fennel seed, garlic, ginger, peppercorns, star anise

FRENCH
garlic, herbes de Provence, nutmeg, rosemary, thyme

INDIAN
cardamom, cayenne, cinnamon, cloves, coriander, cumin, garlic, ginger, mustard seed, turmeric

ITALIAN
basil, garlic, hot pepper, oregano, parsley, rosemary, sage, thyme

KOREAN
black pepper, garlic, ginger, green onion, parsley, red pepper flakes, salt, sesame seeds

MEXICAN
chili powder, cinnamon, coriander, cumin, garlic, oregano

MIDDLE EASTERN
bay leaf, cardamom, cinnamon, cloves, coriander, cumin, ginger, oregano

NORTH AFRICAN
cardamom, cinnamon, cumin, ginger, harissa, paprika, *ras el hanout*, turmeric

THAI
basil, cardamom, cumin, garlic, ginger, lemongrass, turmeric

TURKISH

> allspice, cinnamon, cumin, hot pepper flakes, mint, oregano, paprika, sesame seeds, sumac

WHAT SPICES AND HERBS CAN DO FOR YOUR COOKING

A proverb from the Republic of Georgia attests that when a guest visits, a boring day turns into a holiday. The same could be said for cooking with spices and herbs. They can transform a drab meal into a celebration of the senses. Used deftly, they highlight the flavor of the individual ingredients. Whether you're cooking the last zucchini you grew in your garden or a simple bowl of rice, like a bright scarf transforming an everyday outfit into festive attire, spices and herbs often bring a greater appreciation for the foods themselves.

When we say that something tastes delicious, what we are actually referring to is the smell. Twenty percent of our taste comes from the taste buds on our tongue—about 9,000 of them—that can detect sweet, salt, sour, bitter, and that enigmatic savory-meaty flavor called *umami* in Japanese. Compare this to the five to ten million smell receptors we have in our noses that allow us to distinguish up to 10,000 unique smells. For example, the flavor of anise seed on the tongue tastes sweet, but it contains up to 25 different aromatic compounds.

Molecular gastronomists have been working with the idea that foods containing chemical compounds that trigger the same smell receptors pair well together. For example, jasmine and pork both contain the volatile molecule indole. Therefore, eating these two together tastes good. Other unlikely combinations include mango and violet, oyster and kiwi, cauliflower and cocoa, salmon and licorice, banana and cloves, chipotle and orange, and lavender and coffee. But you don't have to be a molecular gastronomist to start trying new flavor combinations. By experimenting with spices, you can become your own kitchen scientist, infusing your meals with new heights of flavor.

Besides flavor and aroma, spices add texture and color to your dishes. A rub of turmeric, cumin, paprika, cayenne pepper, and chili powder on your grilled chicken not only gives it a lovely tone but crisps the texture of the skin. While herbs are usually green, the golden yellow of turmeric, the bronze of cumin, the rich chestnut of cinnamon, and the deep crimson of paprika can add rich, earthy hues to your food.

Aside from the artistic, a practical reason to use spices is that almost all of them have antioxidant, antifungal, antiviral, and antiparasitic properties, characteristics for which spices were originally valued, particularly in their aforementioned ability to preserve food. They can't cure a specific disease unless used in a higher quantity than typically used in recipes, and under the supervision of a health care provider, but increasing evidence indicates that daily consumption of spices is useful in helping prevent diseases.

Spices and herbs have another capability as well: the power to create and bring back memory. There's a Welsh word, *hiraeth*, which means a type of homesickness for somewhere you cannot return, a nostalgia for lost places or possibly places you've never been. Spices and herbs contain a kind of story within them, and they can bring you back to those lost places or even conjure up places that haven't yet been invented. They can help fabricate an atmosphere of romance, comfort, excitement, and even luxury. Herbal folklore even suggests that some spices help generate certain qualities like love or resilience. Sage, for example, is associated with wisdom; sesame with openness; rosemary with fidelity; hot pepper with passion and vitality; ginger with desire; and cardamom with sweet breath and fresh conversations.

Learning about spices is a little like learning a new language, but a language of the senses that is much easier—and more enjoyable—to comprehend and absorb. In short, spices and herbs can achieve the following:

ADD FLAVOR AND AROMA. Spices can transform a meal by adding a range of delicious, comforting, exotic, or even unusual flavors.

ADD COLOR. Fresh herbs can accentuate a dish with the colors of spring. Spices like turmeric can dye your whole dish yellow.

ADD TEXTURE. As mentioned earlier, a spice rub of turmeric, cumin, paprika, cayenne pepper, and chili powder not only adds a beautiful color to your grilled chicken but gives the skin a slightly crispy texture.

IMPROVE HEALTH. Spices contain antioxidant, antimicrobial, and often anti-inflammatory properties. They are also good substitutes for sugar and salt.

CREATE MEMORY. Perhaps most important, a delicious meal redolent of spices creates olfactory memories, cements friendships, and inspires new ones.

Need-to-Know Spices and Herbs

With hundreds of spices and herbs to choose from, how do you know where to begin? To help you transform and diversify your kitchen, this guide profiles the 50 most important usable spices and herbs so you can start cooking with greater, more evocative flavor.

STOCKING YOUR SPICE RACK

The spices and herbs profiled in chapters 2 and 3 have become easily accessible, but what if you simply don't have room in your spice rack or cupboard for 50 little jars of spices and herbs? Unless you are an avid cook with tons of storage space and ample financial resources, stocking them all isn't very practical.

When choosing which spices to purchase, consider how often you are likely to cook specific regional cuisines. For example, how often are you really going to make that exotic Moroccan dish? Consider the types of food you are most likely to cook, look over the lists of spices in the global kitchen section (here), and choose the ones you are most likely to use. Or simply select some of the following spices, considered the most practical and essential, to get started:

BLACK PEPPER. If you can get whole peppercorns and a pepper grinder, you will notice a significantly more pungent flavor than with preground pepper.

CAYENNE. Add zest or heat to your dishes with cayenne.

CHILI POWDER. Add chili powder to eggs, beans, chili, soups, or any Mexican dish.

CINNAMON. Cinnamon is great for all types of baking. Add it to smoothies and desserts, and keep a little bowl of sugar on hand mixed with a teaspoon of cinnamon to sprinkle on buttered toast.

CUMIN. Cumin is a great addition to stews, rubs, or yogurt sauce for vegetables or fish.

GARLIC POWDER. Though fresh garlic is always preferable, if you don't have time to peel and chop it, a dash of garlic powder will always enhance a savory dish.

PAPRIKA. The great thing about paprika is that its flavor is so subtle, you can add it to almost anything to provide some color without strongly affecting the flavor of the food. Try adding it to eggs, potato dishes, and soups.

SALT. Salt is technically a mineral, rather than a spice. Consider substituting Himalayan crystal salt for white table salt. The flavor is more complex and contains more than 80 healthy trace minerals.

TURMERIC. Add turmeric to salmon while grilling or to soups or sauces for an intensely beautiful color.

When purchasing herbs, first consider which ones might be practical to grow yourself. We recommend using fresh herbs whenever possible, but when not in season, the following dried herbs are always helpful to have on hand:

BAY LEAF. If you don't have a bay laurel tree, it's a good idea to stock up on a few bay leaves, which enhance any soup or stock.

OREGANO. Oregano is good on pizzas and in tomato sauces and stews.

SAGE. A bit of sage can enhance any chicken dish, or sauté it in butter and pour the mixture over ravioli.

TARRAGON. Tarragon is good with eggs, seafood, and poultry.

THYME. Though fresh always trumps dried, a pinch of dried thyme can improve almost any dish.

SPICES AND HERBS AND YOUR HEALTH

A kitchen bursting with aromatic spices roasting in the oven is, in itself, a kind of cure-all, at least emotionally. But according to the World Health Organization, 70 percent of the people on the planet use spices and herbs medicinally for a variety of ailments. Many modern pharmaceuticals are rooted in plant-based medicine, like the willow bark in aspirin. Herbal remedies can help relieve indigestion, break up chest congestion, prevent colds, and alleviate stress, anxiety, inflammation, headaches, cramps, and general malaise. Rich in antioxidants, spices and herbs can also help prevent aging. In addition, they can lower cholesterol, boost protection from heart disease, and help stave off cancer. Spices and herbs can jumpstart your metabolism, stimulate the appetite, and lower blood sugar. Some herbs are even libido boosters and can increase vitality and fertility.

Almost all spices are high in antifungal, antiviral, and antiparasitic properties, but some are more adept at fighting particular viruses and parasites than others. Garlic, for instance, has recently been discovered to prevent antibiotic resistance. Meanwhile, turmeric combats inflammation, and ginger reduces morning sickness. For actual treatment of disease, these spices would have to be taken under the advice of a health care practitioner. However, with daily use, spices can help prevent disease and create a sense of general well-being amidst the daily stresses of life. According to naturopathic doctors, even a teaspoon of Ceylon cinnamon in a morning smoothie can lower blood sugar.

The Indian system of Ayurveda has been using spices for 3,000 years in its healing practices, infusing cloves, turmeric, and cardamom into massage oils. Both Chinese medicine and Ayurveda are founded on the principle that good health depends on balancing the elements of the body. In Chinese medicine each element corresponds to a color (yellow: earth, red: fire, blue: wood, white: metal, and black: water), so the Chinese dietary system recommends eating dishes that contain all the colors. Though it's rare to find a blue spice, the other colors recognized in Chinese medicine are abundant.

For the specific healing properties of each spice or herb, refer to their individual profiles in the following chapters.

STORAGE OF SPICES AND HERBS

Have you ever purchased a big, beautiful bunch of fresh basil, used half of it, and then forgot about it as it slowly turned into black goo in the bottom of the refrigerator? Or, have you ever bought a spice for a dish you were cooking, let it get lost in the back of the cupboard, and ended up buying a second container the next time you needed it? Here are a few tips to help prevent these common snafus from happening again, as well as some general storage advice:

KEEP SPICES AWAY FROM DIRECT SUNLIGHT, MOISTURE, AND HEAT. This means you should also keep spices away from the stove. If you have a drawer or two near your stove, however, this is a useful place to keep your spices, as long as the labels are clearly visible. If you have to rummage around in a cupboard, knocking over spices in the process, you'll be less likely to want to use them when cooking.

STORE YOUR SPICES IN GLASS CONTAINERS (RATHER THAN PLASTIC). If you can find dark or amber glass, that's even better, or store them in tin containers to keep out the light completely. Again, label them clearly, and make sure you have easy access to them.

CHOOSE WHOLE SPICES OVER GROUND. Whole spices maintain their freshness longer than ground. You might want to invest in a mortar and pestle or a coffee grinder that you'll use specifically for spices, and keep it near your spice rack. Though some cooks insist upon cooking with spices as fresh as possible, properly stored, whole spices can last up to four years. Ground spices can last up to three years, and dried herbs for two.

TRY ORGANIZING YOUR SPICE RACK. You could arrange it either alphabetically or according to the spices and herbs most often used together.

STORE PAPRIKA AND OTHER RED PEPPERS IN THE REFRIGERATOR, WHERE THEY'LL STAY FRESH LONGER. Avoid refrigerating other spices with them, though, since the humidity can affect many spices adversely.

CHOP UP AND FREEZE FRESH HERBS. When frozen in ice cube trays, you can remove them, store them in plastic bags, and use just the amount you need when you need it.

DRY YOUR OWN FRESH HERBS. Simply tie them into a bunch and hang them upside down in a dark, dry area with enough air circulation to prevent mold growth. They should be dry within a week. You can leave them hanging and break off bits as needed, or store them in jars.

USE MOISTURE TO KEEP FRESH HERBS LONGER. Store them in a glass of water on the windowsill or wrapped in a wet paper towel, placed in a plastic bag, and placed in the refrigerator.

AVOID STORING YOUR FRESH HERBS IN THE BACK OF THE REFRIGERATOR. It's easy to forget about something that gets lost in the back of the fridge. Keeping fresh herbs visible in the fridge will help ensure that you use them.

WHEN PLANNING YOUR WEEKLY MEALS, CHOOSE RECIPES THAT USE THOSE HERBS MORE THAN ONCE. This is a great way to ensure that those fresh herbs don't go to waste.

GROWING YOUR OWN FRESH HERBS

Adding a sprig of fresh thyme to almost any dish will liven it up, but how often do you have fresh thyme on hand? The good news is that some herbs are really simple to grow. You can grow your own herb garden right on your windowsill. If your windowsill isn't big enough to hold several pots of herbs, you could always build shelves in front of your window and have a three-or-more-tiered herb shelf garden. The beauty of the herbs more than compensates for losing your view out the window.

To grow the herbs, you can either plant the seeds in seed trays or simply buy starter herbs at a nursery. Some supermarkets sell pots of basil. The easiest herbs to grow indoors are thyme, marjoram, basil, dill, summer savory, and lemon balm. (Sipping on a cup of lemon balm tea will relieve any anxiety you are having about your herb garden.) Once your starters have grown, you can put all the little pots of herbs in a basket. For beautiful ideas on how to decorate your house with herb gardens, take a look at some images on Pinterest.

A few herbs like parsley, cilantro, and basil have shorter growing seasons and require a lot of sunlight. Usually they will last only a year, but if you keep them warm through the frost season, they can last for two. Since rosemary has such a pungent smell, it's best to grow it outside, especially since it likes to dig its roots into the ground and grow into a bush large enough to provide your entire neighborhood with fresh rosemary. Lavender is also a lovely plant to grow outside, as is mint, since they will all survive through cold winters.

The hardest part about growing herbs is that they like to be watered every day. For this reason it's helpful to keep them near the sink. If you find that your herbs are growing too abundant, you can tie them into bunches and dry them. They also make great gifts.

TIPS FOR COOKING WITH SPICES AND HERBS

GRIND YOUR WHOLE SPICES. Consider investing in a mortar and pestle or coffee grinder that you can use exclusively for grinding spices. Since exposure to air and sun weakens the spice, buy whole spices and grind them as you need them. This will produce the strongest flavors and most fragrant aromas. Some spices, however, such as cinnamon, coriander, and cumin, are too hard to grind into a very fine powder, so you are better off buying the powdered variety.

SMELL YOUR SPICES. Spices and herbs won't spoil, but if their color isn't as vibrant as you remember, the flavor has likely faded as well. If you can't remember using a spice in a long time, smell and taste it before adding it to your food to make sure it still tantalizes your nose and tongue. The more robust the spice, the less you'll need in your recipe.

KEEP SPICES AWAY FROM STEAM. If you can avoid it, don't sprinkle the spice directly over a pot of boiling water or soup, because the steam can get into the spice and spoil it, or at least clog up the holes in the lid of the jar.

TOAST YOUR SPICES. To open up the flavor and add a nutty quality, try toasting your spices in a dry pan over low heat. Being careful not to burn them, remove them from the pan as soon as you begin to smell the nuttiness. Using this method makes both spices and herbs easier to grind. You can also gently sauté the spices in oil, and then use that oil in cooking, since it will be infused with the flavor of the spice.

USE SPICES AND HERBS SELECTIVELY. Too many cooks in the kitchen spoil the broth, but sometimes too many spices can, too. Use spices selectively until you become familiar with how the spices or herbs complement each other. Add fresh spices during cooking for a more blended flavor, and at the end of cooking for a more defined flavor.

CRUSH FRESH HERBS IN YOUR HAND. Crushing fresh herbs in your hand before adding them to your dish releases the flavor.

CONSIDER COOKING TIME. Whole spices and leaves take longer to release their flavor. Use whole spices, such as cloves or bay leaves, when cooking stews, and use ground spices and herbs for dishes with shorter cooking times.

USE RED PEPPER SPICES MODERATELY. Red pepper spices like cayenne increase in intensity while cooking. Use incrementally to avoid overpowering a recipe with heat.

TRY SPICE MARINADES. In some cultures, adding spices like salt and pepper after cooking is considered the equivalent of painting a flavor onto the dish. Marinating vegetables or meat before cooking can help release the internal flavor of the food.

FRESH VS. DRIED HERBS

The herb profiles in this book focus on fresh herbs. However, since fresh herbs aren't always available, you might try cooking with only those herbs that are in season. When substituting a dried herb for a fresh one, you'll find that the woodier herbs such as rosemary, thyme, or oregano do better than the more tender herbs like basil. As a general rule, it's best not to substitute dried basil, chives, parsley, or dill for the fresh version. For the most complex flavor combination, you can use both fresh and dried varieties of the same herb. Dried herbs have a slightly more bitter taste, whereas fresh herbs are more delicate.

In terms of cooking time, fresh herbs should be added toward the end of cooking to retain their flavor, while dried herbs need to cook longer to avoid tasting woody or dusty. Regarding quantity, since dried herbs are more concentrated than fresh, the general rule is a three-to-one ratio: one teaspoon of dried cilantro would equal three teaspoons (one tablespoon) of fresh cilantro.

It's difficult to believe that people were once willing to pay exorbitant prices and embark on dangerous journeys just for the luxury of flavor. Hopefully, by experimenting with some of the essential spices profiled in this chapter, you will come to understand why this might have been so. Each profile presents the foods it complements, other spices and herbs that pair well with it, plus two sample recipes that feature that spice. All these elements will familiarize you with each spice's many possible flavor combinations so that you can create fragrant dishes of your own.

Allspice

Columbus sailed to America in search of a quicker route to India to acquire spices. When he landed, he called the Native Americans "Indians." When he discovered allspice in Jamaica, he called it "pepper" (later changed to Jamaican pepper). When the English tasted this native spice from Jamaica, they called it allspice because it tasted like a mixture of cinnamon, nutmeg, and cloves, spices they already knew. It seems that the English had difficulty naming things that weren't already familiar! Cinnamon, nutmeg, and cloves, however, *do* resemble allspice, because all these spices, as well as basil and bay leaf, contain the aromatic chemical eugenol, which is also an antiseptic and antimicrobial agent. Allspice is a fruit that, when dried, resembles peppercorns. Efforts at reproduction have been unsuccessful because the seeds germinate only if they have passed through the guts of a bird. The allspice tree now grows in Hawaii and a few Central American countries.

In the Kitchen *One of the main spices used in Caribbean cooking, allspice is best when ground fresh because it can lose its flavor quickly after grinding. The leaves of the allspice tree are similar to bay leaves and can be used as such. In Jamaican jerk dishes, even the wood from the tree is used to smoke meat. The flavor is actually contained in the shell of the allspice seed rather than the seed itself. When ground, allspice can be added to jams and pies as well as sauerkraut and other pickled dishes. Try it sprinkled over a fried banana with vanilla ice cream.*

❉ REGIONAL STAR

Allspice is used to flavor and preserve fish and meat in the Caribbean, where it is pounded into a paste and slathered onto food before grilling. In British cuisine, allspice is used in "mixed spice," with ground coriander seeds, mace, nutmeg, cloves, and cinnamon, for baking. An English pickling spice includes allspice berries, ginger, mustard, mace, peppercorns, whole cloves, and coriander seeds.

✚ HEALING POWER

high in antioxidants, vitamins, and minerals; aids digestion

WHERE TO BUY IT: supermarket, specialty grocery store, online

HOW TO STORE IT: Allspice berries crush easily, so it's better to buy and store them whole. Once ground they quickly lose their flavor, but while whole they can be kept almost indefinitely.

COMPLEMENTS

coconut
Indian curries
jerk chicken
lime

molasses
oranges
pilafs
pineapple upside-down cake
plantains
pumpkins
root vegetables
rum
tropical fruits

PAIRS WELL WITH

---

bay leaf
chili
citrus
cloves
garlic
ginger
marjoram
mustard
rosemary
tamarind

FLAVOR PROFILE: *similar to nutmeg, cinnamon, and cloves; warm and pungent flavor*

Prep time: 15 minutes, plus 1 to 24 hours to marinate | Cook time: 1 hour

Serves 4 *A Jamaican take on traditional bourbon chicken, this recipe substitutes rum, which pairs so well with allspice, for the bourbon. Be sure to use a dark rum rather than a light one. If you don't like heat, keep the Scotch bonnet pepper out, though it's this pepper that endows that characteristic flavor to Jamaican food as well as to Jamaican jerk seasonings. When you fry the chicken, the sugar in the marinade will give it a caramelized quality. Serve over rice with Fried Plantains with Allspice (here).*

1 teaspoon ground ginger
4 ounces soy sauce
3 scallion stalks, chopped
½ cup minced onion
½ cup packed brown sugar
½ cup dark rum
1 teaspoon minced garlic
1 teaspoon ground allspice
Juice of 1 lime
1 Scotch bonnet hot pepper, chopped
2 tablespoons coconut oil
1 whole chicken, cut into pieces

In a medium bowl, stir together the ginger, soy sauce, scallions, onion, brown sugar, rum, garlic, allspice, lime juice, and hot pepper.

In a 13-by-9-inch baking pan, coat the chicken in the marinade.

Cover the dish, refrigerate, and marinate for at least an hour or overnight.

Remove the chicken from the marinade, shake off the seasonings, and set the marinade aside.

Preheat the oven to 350°F.

In a large pan over high heat, heat the coconut oil, and brown the chicken a few pieces at a time.

Place the browned chicken back in the baking dish while you fry the rest of the chicken.

Bake the browned chicken with the marinade for 45 minutes to an hour, until done and tender when cut into.

Serve immediately over rice with Fried Plantains with Allspice (here).

TIP: To make your own simple and quick Jamaican jerk spice blend, mix 2 teaspoons each of cayenne pepper, garlic powder, onion powder, dried thyme, and sugar with 1 teaspoon each of paprika, ground allspice, and black pepper and one-half teaspoon each of nutmeg and cinnamon.

Fried Plantains with Allspice

Prep time: 5 minutes | Cook time: 5 minutes

Serves 4 *Plantains are a cross between a banana and a potato— sweeter than potatoes but starchier than bananas. The unripe ones aren't sweet at all and need to be cooked before being eaten. They take a long time to ripen if you want to try eating them raw. Serve these on the side of rum chicken, or make them with bananas and brown sugar, and serve them over vanilla ice cream for dessert.*

4 ripe plantains, peeled
4 tablespoons coconut oil
½ teaspoon ground cinnamon
½ teaspoon ground allspice

Slice the plantains into ¼-inch rounds.

In a large pan over medium heat, heat the coconut oil.

Fry the plantains until golden brown, 2 to 3 minutes.

In a small bowl, mix together the cinnamon and allspice.

Dust the plantains with the spice mixture, and serve.

TIP: For a dessert version, substitute bananas for plantains, add a little brown sugar to the pan when frying, and serve over ice cream. Since this dish requires a high cooking temperature to fry the plantains, coconut oil is recommended over butter. If you only have butter, try clarifying it first by heating it until all the butter is melted and the milk solids sink to the bottom. Then skim off the clear oil on top. This clarified butter is also known as ghee.

Asafetida

Asafetida's unique flavor blend of onion-garlic-shallot-leek could almost be a sixth flavor, developed specifically for vegetarians, after that savory, meaty fifth flavor of umami, the one for meat-eaters. Asafetida is the dried resin-like gum from the sap of an herbaceous plant related to fennel. Because of its pungent garlic- and dung-like smell, it's commonly called both "food of the gods" and "devil's dung." This might sound off-putting, but when cooked, the smell disappears and the flavor of leeks infuses a dish. Though native to Persia and Armenia and a common spice during the Roman Empire, it was largely forgotten about in Europe once Rome fell, due to its reputation for ruining every dish, likely because cooks didn't know how to use it properly—you need very little. One of the rare spices that came to India *from* the West, asafetida is now primarily used in Indian cooking with turmeric to harmonize the flavors of salty, sweet, sour, bitter, and spicy.

In the Kitchen *Have you ever made an Indian dish that just never quite tasted as authentic as it does at Indian restaurants? Next time try adding a pinch of asafetida. Its slightly repellant aroma goes away after it's cooked, but it's better cooked in ghee than in oil. It can also be used as a condiment, like salt, for those who don't mind the smell, and in Indian chutneys and pickles. Its flavor can overpower, so use it sparingly. If you can find it in whole pieces, try rubbing a piece of it on a griddle or frying pan before use.*

⁛ REGIONAL STAR

Primarily an Indian spice, it's used in vegetarian cooking for Jains, Brahmins, Buddhists, and those who don't use onions or garlic in their food. It's used in chaat masala and sambar powder and added to soups, vegetables, and bean dishes. Afghan chefs use it with salt to cure meat.

✛ HEALING POWER

A tiny bit added to a teaspoon of water and heated over a candle can help with colic. An antimicrobial, it can help heal bronchitis. Used by 60 percent of the population in India as a digestive and to help combat flatulence.

WHERE TO BUY IT: supermarket, specialty grocery store, or Indian market. Because it's so difficult to grind, the most common asafetida is commercially ground with 70 percent rice flour and gum arabic.

HOW TO STORE IT: Its pungent aroma will compromise other spices, so keep it in a tightly sealed container. The solid variety keeps for years, and the powdered for up to a year.

COMPLEMENTS

beans
cabbage

cauliflower
fish
ghee
grains
mushrooms
potatoes
roasted meat
spinach
vegetarian cooking

PAIRS WELL WITH

curry spices

FLAVOR PROFILE: *bitter with notes of garlic, onions, and shallots*

Mulligatawny, or Spicy Pepper Soup

Prep time: 5 minutes | Cook time: 20 minutes

Serves 4 *At once spicy and sour, this simple Indian broth-like soup, perfect on a chilly evening or if you are coming down with a cold, is made primarily of tomato and spices. The asafetida helps blend the spices together. This recipe calls for curry leaves, usually available at Indian markets. If you can't find them, simply leave them out.*

2 tablespoons vegetable or coconut oil
1 tablespoon freshly ground black pepper
1 teaspoon cumin seeds
1 teaspoon mustard seeds
¼ teaspoon ground asafetida
2 whole dried red chiles
4 to 6 curry leaves
1 teaspoon ground turmeric
3 garlic cloves, crushed
1¼ cups tomato juice
Juice of 2 limes
½ cup water
Salt
Cilantro leaves, chopped, for garnish

In a large saucepan over medium-high heat, heat the oil and fry the pepper, cumin, mustard seeds, asafetida, chiles, curry leaves, turmeric, and garlic until the garlic is golden brown, about 2 minutes.

Reduce the heat to medium and add the tomato juice, lime juice, and water, and season with salt.

Bring the soup to a boil, lower the heat, and simmer for 10 minutes.

Pour the soup into 4 bowls, garnish with the cilantro, and serve immediately.

Prep time: 15 minutes | Cook time: 1 hour

Serves 4 *This stew features* moong dal, *which you can find at Indian markets or at health food stores, where they are called mung beans. They resemble tiny green balls. Serve this stew with some cucumbers and yogurt. As it sits, the flavors only continue to improve, so you can make it in advance.*

3 cups water
1½ cups raw green *moong dal* (mung beans)
2 tablespoons ground coriander
1 tablespoon grated fresh ginger
½ cup (1 stick) butter or ghee
1 teaspoon ground cumin
½ teaspoon ground asafetida
1 teaspoon ground cayenne pepper
½ teaspoon ground turmeric
1 teaspoon salt, plus more if needed
1 tablespoon Garam Masala Spice Blend (<u>here</u>**)**
Juice of 1 lemon
Fresh cilantro sprigs, for garnish

In a large pot over high heat, bring the water, *moong dal*, coriander, and ginger to a boil.

Cover and simmer until almost cooked, 45 minutes to an hour. Add more water if necessary. If foam forms on the top, use a large spoon to skim it off.

In a large frying pan, heat the butter. Add the cumin and sauté over medium heat until it begins to crackle. Add the asafetida, cayenne, turmeric, and salt, and stir.

Add the mixture to the cooked dal and stir.

Add the Garam Masala Spice Blend, lemon juice, and more salt if needed.

Garnish with the fresh cilantro and serve with rice.

TIP: Different combinations of spices bring out the flavors of different varieties of lentil. This dal is made with *moong dal*, but try salmon-colored *masoor dal* with tomatoes, celery, carrots, and ground sesame seeds. Some people add dried cherries to dal to add a sweet element. Or add caramelized onion on top by sautéing minced onion in ghee or butter on low heat for about 20 minutes. And of course, your dal will be more aromatic if you roast and grind the spices immediately before preparing this dish.

Caraway

In herbal folklore, caraway was used to create a love tonic to prevent couples from falling out of love. It was also alleged that whatever a person sprinkled with caraway seeds would not get stolen. (Don't try this at home or with your car.) Caraway is actually not a seed but a fruit, and because it has a similar appearance to cumin and fennel, it is often confused with them. It grows best in northern climates where there's lots of light during the summer months, and it's one of the favored spices in Scandinavian and Eastern European cooking. When brewed into a tea, it's useful in fighting colic, intestinal worms, and other digestive disorders. Caraway seeds can be grown in your garden in full sun and well-drained soil, but the fruits won't ripen until the second year. Harvest early in the morning when they are wet, or the seeds will scatter, then hang them upside down in a paper bag to catch the falling fruits.

In the Kitchen *Caraway's flavor characterizes many German, Austrian, and Scandinavian foods. The leaves, which resemble carrot tops, can be eaten like parsley, and the roots are edible, too. Caraway can be used in pickles and sprinkled on top of bagels, rye breads, and crackers, and it pairs well with hazelnuts, mushrooms, and noodles. It's a great addition to pot roasts, sausages, Reuben sandwiches, or a sauté of apples and cabbage, and it can replace parsley in any dish. To make an herbal (or love) tonic, pour a cup of boiling water into a mug containing two tablespoons of pressed seeds, let cool, and drink.*

✳ REGIONAL STAR

In British and German food, caraway is often added to sauerkraut. In the Middle East, a caraway pudding is served during Ramadan. Caraway's essential oil, along with dill, is the main flavoring in the Scandinavian liquor akvavit, or "water of life." It's also one of the main spices in the Tunisian harissa spice blend.

✚ HEALING POWER

excellent source of fiber, vitamins, and minerals; assists in digestive disorders

WHERE TO BUY IT: supermarket, specialty grocery store, online

HOW TO STORE IT: usually sold whole; best not to grind them until ready for use because, like almost all spices, they lose their flavor and healing properties quickly once ground.

COMPLEMENTS

baked goods
breads
cabbage dishes
cheeses

**fish
roast pork
sausages
vegetables
and any dish where parsley is used**

PAIRS WELL WITH

**coriander
garlic
juniper berries
lemon
nutmeg
oranges
parsley
salt
thyme**

FLAVOR PROFILE: *bittersweet; reminiscent of anise and cumin with a hint of dried orange peel*

Cabbage with Apple, Sausage, and Caraway

Prep time: 10 minutes | Cook time: 25 minutes

Serves 4 to 6 *This Eastern European dish highlights the flavor of caraway since, besides salt and pepper, it's the only flavoring agent. Substitute purple cabbage for green, if desired.*

2 tablespoons butter
1½ teaspoons caraway seeds
1 cup chopped onion
2 teaspoons minced garlic
5 cups coarsely shredded green cabbage (1 small head or ½ large head)
1 apple, peeled and cut into slices
1 tablespoon balsamic vinegar (apple cider will also work)
½ cup chicken or vegetable broth
1 pound or Polish kielbasa or other sausage of your choosing
Salt
Freshly ground black pepper

In a frying pan over medium heat, melt the butter. Add the caraway seeds and toast until fragrant, about 2 minutes.

Add the onion and garlic. Cook, stirring occasionally, until soft.

Add the cabbage, apple, vinegar, and broth. Bring to a boil, cover, and simmer for 10 minutes.

Add the kielbasa. Cover and cook for an additional 10 to 15 minutes.

Season with salt and pepper.

Serve by itself, on top of boiled potatoes, or with Caraway Soda Bread (here).

Caraway Soda Bread

Serves 8 (Makes 1 loaf) *Enjoy this simple-to-prepare soda bread hot with butter, Cheddar cheese, jam, or Cabbage with Apple, Sausage, and Caraway (here). It's also delicious with a variety of soups and salads.*

4 cups flour
1 teaspoon baking soda
1 teaspoon salt
1 tablespoon sugar
1½ teaspoons caraway seeds
½ cup butter (cold)
1 large egg
1¾ cups buttermilk

Preheat the oven to 425°F.

Lightly grease a baking sheet.

In a large bowl, mix together the flour, baking soda, salt, sugar, and caraway seeds.

Using a pastry cutter or your fingers, work the butter into the flour mixture until it resembles coarse meal.

Make a hole in the center of the flour and add the egg and buttermilk into it.

Mix until the dough is stiff, and gently knead it until it forms a ball, adding a little extra flour to your hands if needed.

Place the dough on a floured surface and shape it into a round loaf. Try to handle the dough as little as possible, or it may become tough. If it's sticky, add a little more flour to your hands.

Using a serrated knife, cut a cross on the top of the dough.

Bake until the bread is golden brown, 35 to 45 minutes.

Remove the bread from the oven and let it sit in the pan for a few minutes.

Serve warm.

Cardamom

After saffron and vanilla, cardamom is one of the most expensive spices, though not prohibitively so. Cardamom comes from an evergreen tree that originally grew only in the forests of South India, where it has been used for 2,000 years, though Guatemala is now the main producer. Related to the ginger family, cardamom offers ginger's digestive assistance and can help combat heartburn and constipation. As an antispasmodic, it can even get rid of hiccups. Chewing on cardamom freshens the breath and helps prevent oral infections. It is also known to be an aphrodisiac. In Chaucer's *The Canterbury Tales*, cardamom was called "the spice of paradise." In the Middle East it's added to coffee as a sign of respect to guests. The three types of cardamom are the bleached white variety, the smokier black cardamom, and the golden-green pods, each containing about 20 highly aromatic seeds. The stickier the seeds, the fresher they are.

In the Kitchen *Cardamom pods can be added to rice or meat dishes in the same way you would use bay leaf (more flavor is extracted if you crush the pods first), or the seeds can be added whole or ground to desserts or beverages like Turkish coffee or Indian chai. Add cardamom to apples and cabbage; mix it into a rice pilaf with raisins, rosewater, and saffron; or add it to roast duck, specialty ice creams, custards, and even pickles.*

REGIONAL STAR

In Scandinavia, cardamom is used more than cinnamon to spice breads, cakes, and pastries. In India, cardamom is mixed with curry leaves, garlic, ginger, and turmeric in masalas, dals, and pilafs. Green cardamom is used primarily for sweeter dishes, and black cardamom, which has a more intense and smoky flavor, is only used for savory dishes. Cardamom is also one of the essential ingredients in berbere, an Ethiopian spice blend.

HEALING POWER

antispasmodic, digestive, freshens breath

WHERE TO BUY IT: supermarket, specialty grocery store

HOW TO STORE IT: Cardamom seeds left in their pod will last a few years and still retain their potency.

COMPLEMENTS

almonds
baked pears
black beans
butter
caramel
chocolate
coconut

coffee
custards
dates
fruit
pastries
pistachios
rice
sweet potatoes
tea

PAIRS WELL WITH

---

chai
cinnamon
cloves
coffee
flourless chocolate cake
honey
lemon
mint
orange

FLAVOR PROFILE: *Green cardamom has flowery aromas of lemon, peppery pine, and sweet eucalyptus. Black cardamom is smokier.*

Cardamom Coffee

Prep time: 1 minute | Cook time: 3 minutes

Serves 1 *In some Middle Eastern countries, it is a sign of respect to show the guests the cardamom they are about to be served in their coffee. Each country has its own secrets to Turkish coffee—and its own method of how to read the coffee grounds left at the bottom of the cup. Many cooks insist that you must boil the coffee three times. This might be because the Turkish coffee available to them is of lesser quality and often more dried out than the coffee the West has become accustomed to, which might account for the fact that they can drink many cups of Turkish coffee a day.*

1 cup water
2 teaspoons Turkish coffee or finely ground coffee
1 teaspoon sugar
¼ teaspoon ground cardamom or 4 pods green cardamom

Pour the water into the smallest pot you have, or into a Turkish coffee pot.

Add the coffee, sugar, and cardamom, and stir.

Bring to a full boil, remove from the heat, and serve immediately.

TIP: The freshly ground coffee we can get has a higher caffeine content and more pungent flavor than Turkish coffee, which you can find at Middle Eastern markets or online. Try experimenting with different types of coffees. Many Turkish coffees are very sweet, so adjust the sugar according to personal taste.

Cardamom-Ginger–Marinated Lamb Chops with Mint-Pistachio Salsa

Prep time: 15 minutes, plus 2 to 24 hours to marinate | Cook time: 8 to 10 minutes

Serves 4 to 6 *This simpler-than-it-looks recipe highlights the fragrant and sweet aroma of cardamom. It's delicious alone or on couscous. For a decadent flavor combination, try it topped with this mint-pistachio salsa and a salad made with yogurt, tomato, and cumin.*

FOR THE MARINADE
1 cup thick, full-fat yogurt
5 garlic cloves, minced
1 teaspoon freshly grated ginger
2 tablespoons ground cardamom
½ teaspoon ground cinnamon
¼ teaspoon ground nutmeg
1 teaspoon ground cumin

FOR THE LAMB
2 racks of lamb, cut into chops
1 tablespoon extra-virgin olive oil
1 tablespoon salt
1 tablespoon freshly ground black pepper

FOR THE MINT-PISTACHIO SALSA
⅔ cup pistachios
⅔ cup chopped fresh mint
¼ cup extra-virgin olive oil
2 tablespoons finely chopped red onion
1 teaspoon orange zest

Salt

TO MAKE THE MARINADE
In a large bowl, stir together the yogurt, garlic, ginger, cardamom, cinnamon, nutmeg, and cumin.

TO PREPARE THE LAMB
On a large platter, coat the lamb with the olive oil, salt, and pepper.

Add the lamb to the marinade and coat it thoroughly.

Refrigerate the lamb and marinate for 2 to 24 hours.

TO MAKE THE MINT-PISTACHIO SALSA
In a food processor, coarsely chop the pistachios, mint, olive oil, red onion, and orange zest, and season with salt. Set aside.

TO COOK THE LAMB
Heat the grill or a grill to medium-high heat.

Grill the lamb on one side for about 3 minutes and on the other side for about 5 minutes, until the lamb is cooked through.

Serve with the mint-pistachio salsa.

TIP: If the lamb is medium-rare, it will give when you press the meat with your finger. If it doesn't give, it's well done.

Cayenne

Red Pepper Flakes

Every culture uses some variety of chile pepper: Thai, banana, Korean, Jamaican hot, Scotch bonnet, and tabasco, to name a few. Mexico uses the widest variety—serrano, jalapeño, habanero, chilaca, cascabel, chipotle, ancho, and guajillo—and creates dishes with some of the most complex chile pepper flavor combinations. Many of these hot peppers can be found at your local supermarket, and when used fresh, they can add a different character to your dishes than when dry. Generally speaking, the smaller the pepper, the hotter it is, with the seeds delivering the spiciest kick. The dried red pepper most commonly found in the spice section of your local supermarket is the cayenne pepper. Like the peppers making up the spice, paprika, the cayenne pepper comes from the *Capsicum annuum* plant. But while paprika is a blend of many peppers ranging from mild to hot, the cayenne spice comes from a single pepper—a blazing hot one. Red pepper flakes come from the same pepper but are used more as a condiment.

In the Kitchen *Try sprinkling cayenne on corn or tropical fruit for a Mexican street-food treat. Use it in a spice mixture to add to nuts, in bean chilies or mashed potatoes, or sprinkled over sautéed mushrooms with some garlic, onions, and a little cream and sherry. The ground version of cayenne pepper is best added to soups and broths to spread its flavor and color throughout, as in a Mexican tortilla chicken soup.*

REGIONAL STAR
Dried pepper flakes, which include both the dried fruits and seeds, are found on the tables in Hungary, Turkey, the Middle East, and in pizza restaurants in North America. These are usually added after the meal has been cooked, for extra zing. Cayenne pepper (and other spicy red peppers) is essential to chili powders, curry powders, harissa, jerk seasoning, kimchi, moles, and sambals.

HEALING POWER
Cayenne is rich in vitamins and minerals, but since you use only a small amount, there are more efficient ways to get vitamins. The high levels of capsaicin boost metabolism, which can aid in weight loss. Cayenne can also help stave off colds and the flu, aid in digestion by producing more saliva, relieve joint pain, and increase blood circulation. The capsicum of cayenne pepper can also be found in topical creams, though putting a cayenne pepper directly on a wound is not recommended. A cayenne pepper weight-loss drink combining maple syrup, cayenne pepper, water, and lemon juice was trending a few years ago. The reason it might have worked is that cayenne pepper acts as a diuretic, purging the colon of excess waste, though given the spiciness of cayenne, it probably isn't a comfortable process. Cayenne pepper does reduce appetite and make you feel full.

WHERE TO BUY IT: supermarket, specialty grocery store, online

HOW TO STORE IT: away from heat and moisture. Fresh peppers can be stored in oil.

COMPLEMENTS

---

   almonds
   beans
   cashews
   chocolate
   corn
   eggs
   jambalaya
   lemon
   lentils
   mushrooms
   pine nuts
   potatoes
   sour cream
   vinegar
   walnuts

PAIRS WELL WITH

---

   cumin
   dill
   garlic
   sugar

FLAVOR PROFILE: *pungent, hot, musty with notes of tobacco*

Prep time: 5 minutes | Cook time: 10 minutes

Serves 2 Puttanesca *means brothel, and this pasta is named for it because it will keep you up all night. This flavorful dish uses hot pepper flakes instead of cayenne. In addition to being spicy, this dish is quite salty, so to cut the salt a little, serve it with a bottle of red wine.*

- **6 to 8 ounces spaghetti**
- **2 tablespoons extra-virgin olive oil**
- **1 teaspoon red pepper flakes (or more if desired)**
- **1 (1.6-ounce) can anchovies, chopped**
- **5 garlic cloves, minced**
- **4 tablespoons tomato paste**
- **2 tablespoons capers (and a little of the juice)**
- **½ cup Kalamata olives**
- **2 ounces grated fresh Parmesan cheese**
- **Freshly ground black pepper**

In a large pot over high heat, boil the amount of water indicated by the spaghetti package directions, and add the spaghetti.

While the spaghetti is boiling for the time indicated by the package directions, heat the olive oil in a pan over medium-high heat.

Add the pepper flakes until they start to pop; then add the anchovies and garlic and stir for a minute or two.

Add the tomato paste and fry for about a minute, stirring continuously.

Add the capers, caper juice, olives, and a little water until the mixture reaches a sauce-like consistency. Reduce the heat to low.

Check to see if the spaghetti is done. (You could throw it against the wall. If it sticks, the spaghetti is done. Or just taste it.)

When the spaghetti is done, drain it and divide it between 2 plates.

Pour the sauce over the hot spaghetti, and serve immediately with the Parmesan cheese and black pepper. (If the olives still have pits, be sure to warn your guest.)

TIP: Cayenne's heat increases in strength the longer it's cooked, so use this spice with caution. When grinding this or other dried peppers at home, be sure to wear a mask and avoid touching your eyes. If your hands begin to burn, rub them with cold yogurt; similarly, if your tongue is burning—eating some yogurt will put out the fire. Water only makes it worse.

Spicy Cayenne-Roasted Nuts

Prep time: 5 minutes | Cook time: 25 minutes

Makes 3 cups *These spicy nuts are a great party food. If you're on a low-salt diet, they provide plenty of flavor without the salt. Try adding dried banana chips and/or raisins as well for a trail mix, after roasting the nuts.*

1½ teaspoons sugar
1 teaspoon ground cumin
1 teaspoon ground paprika
1 teaspoon ground cayenne pepper
½ teaspoon garlic powder
¼ teaspoon ground allspice or cloves (optional)
3 cups raw cashews, almonds, peanuts, pecans, hazelnuts, walnuts, or any combination of these
½ cup pumpkin seeds (optional)
½ cup sunflower seeds (optional)
3 tablespoons extra-virgin olive oil
Salt

Preheat the oven to 300°F.

In a small bowl, mix together the sugar, cumin, paprika, cayenne, garlic, and allspice.

In a large bowl, mix together the nuts and seeds (if using).

Add the spice mixture and olive oil, and stir until the nuts and seeds (if using) are well coated.

Spread the mixture onto 2 baking sheets.

Bake for 20 to 25 minutes, stirring occasionally, until the nuts begin to brown.

Season with salt and let cool on the baking sheets.

Store in an airtight container.

TIP: To make your own chili powder blend, mix together 2 tablespoons paprika, 2 teaspoons oregano, 2 teaspoons cumin, and ½ to 2 teaspoons cayenne pepper, depending on the degree of spice you like. Alternatively, for a smokier chili powder, find a variety of dried red chiles, like ancho chiles, cascabel chiles, and árbol chiles, and roast them over a dry pan for 4 to 5 minutes (keeping your face away). Let them cool, and grind them with the rest of the spices. Sprinkle this blend on beans, rice, eggs, or chili, or simply add the powder to your table as a condiment.

Cinnamon

Cinnamon is one of the oldest spices known to humankind. Powerful in preservative properties, it was, like many other spices, even used as an embalming agent. It's important to know that there are actually two types of cinnamon. The more common variety comes from the inner bark of the cassia tree grown in Indonesia and Vietnam and is probably the one you have in your cupboard. The second variety, native to Sri Lanka and known as Ceylon cinnamon, is the cinnamon recently recognized for its ability to lower blood sugar and fight diabetes. A half-teaspoon a day can even lower cholesterol. Ceylon cinnamon has a sweeter, more delicate flavor than cassia cinnamon, which is slightly more astringent. So if you can find it, choose Ceylon cinnamon over the cassia variety. A useful fact about both types, however, is that they are a deterrent for ants—a little cinnamon sprinkled in their path will make them change course.

In the Kitchen *The warming characteristics of cinnamon make it an excellent winter spice for baking during the holidays. The aroma alone boosts brain activity. Cinnamon sticks can be added whole to hot cider, mulled wine, or rice. You can add ground cinnamon to ginger, allspice, cardamom, nutmeg, and cloves for a pumpkin pie spice blend, which you can add to additional desserts like dried figs, prunes, fried bananas, or baked figs with port. And cinnamon is not just for sweet dishes. Add it to braised meats, pickles, sweet potatoes, beans, and squash.*

REGIONAL STAR

Add cinnamon with onions, ginger, garlic, and almonds for a simple and delicious Indian chicken curry, or dust it on top of a spicy Moroccan *bistilla*. Mexico imports cinnamon to add to hot chocolate. Cinnamon accompanies many Iranian stews as well as Indian masalas and chutneys, while cassia cinnamon is used in the Chinese five-spice powder blend to cook meat and chicken.

HEALING POWER

acts as an anti-inflammatory, lowers blood sugar and cholesterol, helps prevent tooth decay, fights cancer, enhances mood

WHERE TO BUY IT: supermarket, specialty grocery store, online

HOW TO STORE IT: Cinnamon sticks, also called quills, can last two to three years if stored away from air and moisture. Ground cinnamon loses its flavor quickly.

COMPLEMENTS

apples
baked goods
chocolate
coffee

curries
figs
lamb
mulled wine
oranges
pears
port
poultry
prunes
rice
squash
sweet potatoes

PAIRS WELL WITH

allspice
cardamom
cloves
ginger
mace
nutmeg
turmeric

FLAVOR PROFILE: *sweet, warm, and spicy with citrus notes*

Prep time: 15 minutes | Cook time: 55 minutes

Serves 8 *Naturopathic doctor Allison Siebecker offers this gluten-free, but cinnamon-and-spice–rich, pumpkin pie recipe. She claims that the cinnamon will prevent any sugar rush from the honey. If you're not avoiding gluten, you can also just use a ready-made crust —though this gluten-free one is delicious!*

FOR THE GLUTEN-FREE SHORTBREAD CRUST
1½ cups blanched almond flour
3 tablespoons butter, melted
2 tablespoons clover honey (according to Allison, clover honey is the best variety for baking)
1 teaspoon baking soda
¼ teaspoon salt
½ cup toasted walnuts, finely chopped (optional)

FOR THE FILLING
1½ cups pumpkin (canned or fresh)
¼ cup butter
½ cup clover honey
3 eggs, beaten
1 tablespoon ground cinnamon
1 teaspoon ground ginger
1 teaspoon ground nutmeg
½ teaspoon ground cloves
Whipped cream, for garnish

TO MAKE THE GLUTEN-FREE SHORTBREAD CRUST
Preheat the oven to 350°F.

In a large bowl, mix together the almond flour, butter, honey, baking soda, salt, and walnuts (if using).

Press the mixture into a 9-inch pie pan.

Bake for 7 minutes.

TO MAKE THE FILLING
Preheat the oven to 250°F.

In a blender, blend together the pumpkin, butter, honey, eggs, cinnamon, ginger, nutmeg, and cloves until smooth.

Pour the mixture into the crust and bake for 40 to 45 minutes.

Serve chilled, topped with whipped cream.

TIP: This pie can also be baked without a crust. In that case, bake it for 38 minutes. To use fresh pumpkin, simply cut the pumpkin into wedges and bake the pumpkin, covered in aluminum foil, in a 375°F oven for an hour, or until soft, and then mash it up. If you wish to serve this pie with whipped cream, try sweetening it with maple syrup and adding a little nutmeg.

Banana-Cinnamon Smoothie

Prep time: 5 minutes

Serves 1 or 2 *This quick, satisfying morning smoothie will energize you until lunchtime. For a colder drink, add a few ice cubes before blending. Or peel the bananas, wrap them in aluminum foil, and freeze them beforehand.*

1 cup milk (or substitute almond, soy, rice, or coconut milk)
½ cup Greek yogurt (fat-free or regular)
2 bananas
1 teaspoon ground cinnamon, plus more for garnish
½ teaspoon vanilla

In a blender, blend together the milk, yogurt, bananas, cinnamon, and vanilla.

Pour into 1 or 2 glasses and serve with a sprinkle of cinnamon on top.

TIP: Try substituting 1 cup of frozen berries for the bananas.

Cloves

One of the most expensive spices during medieval times, cloves were described by the Italian poet Dante Alighieri as what "frivolous squanderers from the town of Siena" use to embellish their meat. Cloves originally derived from a family of the myrtle tree native to Indonesia. The clove is actually the bud of a flower harvested before it opens, keeping all that aromatic fragrance and flavor inside. The pungent aroma can be smelled from afar, and legend has it the scent of cloves is what originally attracted sailors to the Spice Islands. The chemical eugenol, also found in nutmeg, cinnamon, basil, and bay leaf, is what gives cloves their characteristic fragrance. Chinese couriers used to chew on cloves to sweeten their breath, and it's still mixed with tobacco in some cigarettes. Regarding medicinal properties, cloves' numbing effect is useful in treating toothaches, and in Chinese medicine, a topical application over the stomach is thought to warm and stimulate the digestive tract.

In the Kitchen *During the medieval ages, cloves were one of the most important spices used to flavor meat. Their taste can easily overpower all other flavors in a dish, though, so be sure to use them sparingly. Cloves are used in sweet dishes and baked goods such as pumpkin and apple pies, as well as commercially in preparing ketchup and Worcestershire sauces. Leave the cloves whole to flavor mulled wines or preserves; poke into baked apples, onions, or ham and glaze with brown sugar; or add to lentil soup. They also pair with root vegetables like sweet potatoes and beets.*

✳ REGIONAL STAR

In Mexican cuisine, cloves pair well with cinnamon and cumin, and in French cuisine, with pepper, nutmeg, and ginger. An important ingredient in the garam masalas of India and the five-spice mixture of China, cloves also complement the savory meat and rice dishes of North Africa. In Europe they are primarily used as a pickling spice.

✚ HEALING POWER

numbs toothaches and helps prevent gum disease

WHERE TO BUY IT: supermarket, specialty grocery store, online

HOW TO STORE IT: Stored whole, cloves can last a long time in an airtight container; once ground, they lose their medicinal power after a few days.

COMPLEMENTS

apples
beef
beets
chocolate
onion
orange

**pork
poultry
red cabbage
red wine
sweet potatoes**

PAIRS WELL WITH

**basil
cardamom
cinnamon
citrus peel
ginger
pepper
star anise
vanilla**

FLAVOR PROFILE: *fruity and hot with a hint of camphor and pepper*

Mulled Wine

Prep time: 10 minutes | Cook time: 20 minutes

Serves about 12 *Called* glögg *in the Nordic nations and* Glühwein *in Germany, this hot, spiced wine has been consumed throughout the winter and over the holidays for centuries. It was originally brewed to show off not just the wealth of a medieval household, with their access to spices, but the depth of their generosity, so it's ironic we've come to think of this holiday beverage as a way to use up cheap wine. Making a syrup with the spices before adding the wine will allow the spice flavors to blend together to form a mixture that will warm both your kitchen and your conversations.*

2 oranges
Peel of 1 lemon
7 whole cloves, plus 12 more for garnish
5 cardamom pods
2 sticks cinnamon, bruised
½ cup sugar
Pinch ground nutmeg
½-inch peeled ginger knob, cut into quarters
2 bottles not-too-dry red wine

Using a grater, zest the peels of the oranges and the lemon peel. Set the zest aside. Break the oranges into sections.

Stud each piece of orange section with a clove and set aside.

To a large pot, add the orange zest, lemon zest, 7 cloves, cardamom, cinnamon, sugar, nutmeg, and ginger.

Add enough wine to cover the sugar, heat slowly, and stir until the sugar has dissolved.

Bring to a boil and cook for 5 to 7 minutes, until the mixture reaches a syrupy consistency.

Add the rest of the wine and heat until hot but not boiling.

Serve immediately in glasses, adding a clove-garnished orange segment to each.

TIP: For a more intense version, add ¼ cup of brandy. Some people add the flesh of the orange or lemon into the syrup, but this can interfere with the flavor of the wine. Avoid dry wines. Cabernet, Zinfandel, or Merlot are the best wines to use. For a slightly less sweet version, try using less sugar.

Prep time: 15 minutes | Cook time: 1 hour, 30 minutes

Serves 6 to 8 *This book would not be complete without a recipe illustrating why medieval cooks so coveted spices. Here is a recipe for a medieval meat pie. Many meat tarts also included cheese, which has been left out here to highlight the flavors of cloves and meat instead.*

1½ pounds meat (beef, pork, venison, lamb, poultry, or any combination)
3 hard-boiled eggs
Splash red or white wine
1½ cups combination of any of the following: minced dates, currants, raisins, minced figs, chopped almonds, walnuts, onions, parsley, parboiled carrots
½ to 1 cup chicken broth
½ teaspoon salt
½ teaspoon freshly ground black pepper
½ teaspoon ground cloves
¼ teaspoon ground cardamom
½ teaspoon ground cinnamon
½ teaspoon ground ginger
¼ teaspoon ground allspice
Pinch ground nutmeg
Cooked chicken pieces (wings, thighs, etc.) (optional)
9-inch pie shell (lid optional)

In a large pot, boil the meat for 30 minutes, until done. Reserve ⅔ cup of the cooking water.

Preheat the oven to 350°F.

On a platter, cool the meat, then remove it from the bone and chop into small pieces.

In a large bowl, mix together the meat; eggs; wine; broth; combination of fruit, nuts, herbs, and/or vegetables; salt; pepper; cloves; cardamom; cinnamon; ginger; allspice; and nutmeg.

Put the mixture in the pie shell and top with the cooked chicken pieces (if using) and additional pastry crust (if using).

Bake for 45 minutes to an hour, or until the pastry is golden brown and the filling set.

Serve hot or cold.

TIP: The medieval person was famous for eating anything that had wings, and even though the modern cook does not often combine beef with chicken, the medieval cook had no qualms about this. The addition of chicken, or even pheasant, will make this dish the most traditional.

Coriander

Coriander is one of those plants that are both a seed and an herb. The fresh leaves are often called Chinese parsley, and in North American cooking, the fresh herb is usually called cilantro—the Spanish name—because of its ubiquity in Mexican cooking. We are giving the seed of this plant its own profile because its flavor and usage is so different from that of the leaf. Coriander seed is one of the oldest spices known to humankind (references in the Bible compare it to manna from heaven). It is the most widely used and, like so many other spices, was found in King Tut's tomb. Also like many other spices, it contains phytochemicals, antimicrobials helpful in preventing food (and people) from spoiling. Coriander is an annual, meaning it completes its life cycle in one year, though the Egyptians considered it an important plant to eat in the afterlife.

In the Kitchen *Roasting coriander seeds brings out their pungency, though they are delicious fresh, too. Add coriander seeds to the poaching water or brine for fish, or put them in a pepper mill to grind onto your dishes. Coriander is also good in spinach, sautéed with fresh garlic, ginger, and cumin. Add it to stewed fruit or even peanut brittle. In pickles, it gives a sweet, sour flavor.*

☼ REGIONAL STAR

One of the essential spices in South Indian sambar and rasam, coriander seeds are roasted and even eaten as a snack. When ground with cumin, they can act as a thickener in curries. Coriander is also blended with cumin in Mexican dishes. German sausage makers add the seeds to their sausages. North Africans add it to the spice mixtures of harissa and *ras el hanout*, while in Eastern Europe, coriander seeds are sometimes substituted for caraway in rye bread. With orange peel, it's used to add citrus tones to types of Belgian beer.

✛ HEALING POWER

high in dietary fiber, calcium, selenium, iron, magnesium, manganese, vitamin K, and vitamin C; known for its antidiabetic and anti-inflammatory properties; contains digestive enzymes; helps prevent menstrual irregularities; cures conjunctivitis; and can relieve painful joints and hemorrhoids

WHERE TO BUY IT: supermarket, specialty grocery store

HOW TO STORE IT: Ground coriander quickly loses its pungency, so it is best ground fresh. Unlike most other spices, coriander seeds become more pungent as they age.

COMPLEMENTS

apples
beets
chicken

**citrus
fish
lentils
peas
plums
pork
potatoes**

PAIRS WELL WITH

**cinnamon
cloves
cumin
fennel
garlic
ginger
turmeric**

FLAVOR PROFILE: *warm, nutty, and spicy with tones of citrus, sage, and pine forest*

Prep time: 15 minutes | Cook time: 30 minutes

Serves 3 or 4 *This traditional Indian fish curry from Goa uses pomfret, a fish native to the Indian Ocean. You can buy frozen pomfret in Asian markets, or you can substitute sea bass. The curry paste uses plenty of whole red chiles and coriander seeds. Like most Goan cooking, it's delicious but blazing hot. Coconut milk mellows the chili slightly, but to produce a less hot dish, simply use fewer chiles. Serve this fish in its sauce over rice.*

1⅔ pounds pomfret
10 whole red chiles
7 teaspoons coriander seeds
1¾ teaspoons cumin seeds
1½ teaspoons roughly chopped garlic
2 teaspoons peeled and roughly chopped ginger
1 tablespoon tamarind, seeded (if you can't find tamarind, use lemon juice with ½ teaspoon brown sugar)
½ cup extra-virgin olive oil
⅓ cup chopped onion
¼ cup chopped tomatoes
2 cups coconut milk, divided
4 green serrano or other small, hot chiles, seeded
Salt

Clean and wash the fish.

In a blender, blend together the chiles, coriander, cumin, garlic, ginger, and tamarind with enough water, about ½ cup, to make a fine paste.

In a large, heavy saucepan over medium heat, heat the olive oil.

Add the onion and sauté until golden brown.

Add the tomatoes and the paste, and cook for 2 minutes.

Add 1 cup of coconut milk and bring to a boil.

Add the fish and green chiles, and simmer for 5 minutes.

Add the remaining cup of coconut milk and bring to a boil. Remove from the heat.

Serve with rice.

TIP: It's advisable to use a mask while mixing the red chiles and avoid touching your eyes after handing the green and red chiles.

Coriander Spritzer

Prep time: 1 minute, plus 1 day to soak

Serves 1 *This tonic can be used as a digestive aid, a detoxifier, an immunity booster, and a menstrual regulator. Enjoy its warm, spicy flavor hot on a chilly evening.*

Handful coriander seeds
2 cups water
Lemon slices (optional)

Soak the coriander seeds in water for a day.

Remove the seeds, add the lemon slices (if using), and drink.

Alternatively, boil the seeds in water and drink warm.

TIP: For menstrual regulation, drink three times a day. For additional joint relief, add 1 teaspoon fenugreek seeds and 1 teaspoon turmeric.

Cumin

Like pepper, cumin was sometimes used to pay taxes and tithes to priests. Originally from Egypt (another example of those mummy-embalming spices found in King Tut's tomb), it also could be grown in the Mediterranean, North Africa, and the Americas. Because it could grow in the Greek and Roman empires, it was easier to obtain than black pepper, and during the Middle Ages, cumin became a common substitute. It was considered a symbol of love and fidelity, and wedding guests would keep some in their pockets. In Middle Eastern countries, an aphrodisiac was made from a paste of cumin, honey, and black pepper. In Sanskrit, cumin is known as *jeera*, meaning "that which helps digestion." Southern Indians prepare a drink called *jal jeera* by boiling water with cumin seeds. Black cumin seeds, smaller and darker than regular cumin, are often confused with nigella, which looks similar to cumin but has a flavor resembling oregano.

In the Kitchen *Whether the Arabic aphrodisiac paste of cumin, black pepper, and honey actually works is questionable, but the mixture does taste good on chicken and fish. A sauce made from yogurt, mayonnaise, salt, pepper, and cumin also complements fish, as well as steamed vegetables like broccoli. To transform rice, try adding cumin, apricots, and almonds.*

❊ REGIONAL STAR

Cumin is the main condiment spice on the table in Morocco and the base of many spice blends throughout the Middle East and Turkey. In Syria and the countries of the Caucasus, a sauce is made with cumin, pomegranates, and walnuts. Cumin is central to the many kormas and masalas of India, too. *Gobi matar*, an Indian dish made with cauliflower, can contain as much as 5 teaspoons. It's added to beans in Mexican cooking with cilantro and to Tex-Mex chili con carne. Cumin is also an essential base to Cajun spice blends.

✚ HEALING POWER

Cumin's ability to stimulate the secretion of pancreatic enzymes gives it a reputation as a digestive aid. It may also be a liver detoxifier. Two teaspoons of cumin seeds provide almost a fifth of the daily recommended requirement of iron. In Ayurveda, cumin is considered a cooling spice.

WHERE TO BUY IT: supermarket, specialty grocery store. You can find black cumin in Asian markets.

HOW TO STORE IT: Whole cumin keeps for several months, ground cumin for much less. Buy it whole and grind it before use for the best flavor.

COMPLEMENTS

avocados

beans
bulgur
cabbage
cheese
cilantro
dates
eggplant
eggs
hummus
lamb
lemon
mushrooms
onions
peppers
pomegranate
pretzels
sesame seeds
squash
walnuts

PAIRS WELL WITH

---

allspice
bay leaf
cayenne
coriander
fenugreek
ginger
mint
mustard seeds
oregano
turmeric

FLAVOR PROFILE: *nutty, earthy, heady, warm, and spicy*

Moroccan Chicken

Prep time: 15 minutes | Cook time: 1 hour, 20 minutes

Serves 4 *This delicious and aromatic chicken combines the spiciness of cumin with the sweetness of dates. You can also substitute prunes for the dates. Serve with yogurt and Harissa Paste (here).*

2 tablespoons extra-virgin olive oil
3½ pounds chicken, cut into pieces
1 tablespoon ground cumin
1 tablespoon sea salt
1 tablespoon freshly ground black pepper
2 teaspoons dried thyme
3 bay leaves, crushed
4 tablespoons chopped flat-leaf parsley
½ cup green Moroccan olives, pitted or unpitted
12 large dates or prunes
⅓ cup capers, with some of the juice
1½ cups dry red wine
⅓ cup red wine vinegar
⅓ cup brown sugar
½ teaspoon hot red pepper flakes

Preheat the oven to 375°F.

In a large pan over medium-high heat, heat the olive oil.

When hot, add the chicken and brown on both sides, 4 to 5 minutes total.

Place the browned chicken pieces in a 9-by-13-inch baking pan.

In a small bowl, mix together the cumin, salt, pepper, and thyme, and sprinkle the mixture over the chicken.

Add the bay leaves, parsley, olives, dates, and capers to the dish.

Pour the wine and vinegar over the chicken, and sprinkle with the brown sugar and pepper flakes.

Cover the pan with aluminum foil and bake for an hour to an hour and 15 minutes.

Serve over couscous with yogurt and Harissa Paste (here). (If the olives, dates, or prunes still have pits, be sure to warn your guests.)

TIP: Couscous is very easy to make. Use 1½ cups of water for each cup of dry couscous. Boil the water and add it to the couscous with a dash of salt and a teaspoon of extra-virgin olive oil, if desired. Stir it once, cover, and let it sit for 10 minutes. Fluff with a fork before serving.

Cumin-Crusted Carrots and Cauliflower

Prep time: 10 minutes | Cook time: 20 minutes

Serves 3 or 4 *This simple recipe demonstrates how well cumin accompanies cauliflower and root vegetables. You can also substitute potatoes, beets, or parsnips, though they require longer cooking times. For a delicious dressing on steamed cauliflower, simply mix orange juice, honey, olive oil, cumin, salt, and freshly ground black pepper.*

**1 head cauliflower
2 carrots
2 tablespoons extra-virgin olive oil
1 teaspoon ground cumin
1 teaspoon chili powder
1 teaspoon ground paprika
Salt
Freshly ground black pepper**

Preheat the oven to 450°F.

Cut the cauliflower into florets and the carrots into thin slices, about a ¼-inch thick.

Transfer the vegetables into a bowl and coat with the olive oil.

In another small bowl mix the cumin, chili powder, paprika, salt, and pepper.

Coat the vegetables with the spice mixture and spread them onto a 12-inch baking sheet.

Bake for about 20 minutes, and serve.

TIP: To make a yogurt dip for cauliflower, broccoli, or even fish, mix ½ cup of yogurt, 2 tablespoons freshly squeezed lemon juice, and 1 teaspoon cumin, and season with salt and freshly ground black pepper.

Curry Leaves

When the Brits pronounced "Mumbai," it sounded like "Bombay" to them, so they changed the name. Likewise, if you repeatedly pronounce *kari patta*, the Hindi name for curry leaves, it sounds like "curry powder," but curry powder and curry leaves are in fact quite different. Curry leaves come from the leaves of the rue tree, which is native to India and Sri Lanka. These aromatic leaves are reminiscent of curry powder's flavor but lack its spiciness. The leaves are technically the sweeter, more citrusy form of bitter neem leaves. Curry leaves are used in South and West Coast Indian cooking as universally as cilantro in North Indian cooking. Because the dried leaves have virtually no taste, many Indian families have a tree growing in their garden so they can pick a few leaves to immediately add to a dish. Curry leaves resemble the look of bay leaves but can be eaten and are quite healthy.

In the Kitchen *To release the flavor, bruise the leaves first. Curry leaves are best added either at the end of cooking or at the beginning, fried in oil with chopped onion and mustard seeds. They can also be tempered in oil and poured over cooked lentils for a final flavor boost. The crushed leaves flavor chutneys, while the whole leaves are added to pickling spices. Try them fried with onions and a little asafetida in chopped tomatoes and corn, or add them to scrambled eggs or a baked potato.*

⁘ REGIONAL STAR

In Kerala, curry leaves are added to sour tamarind soups, fish curries, and to jackfruit or bitter gourd with coconut, mustard seeds, and turmeric. In other parts of South India, they are also commonly added with cumin seeds and onions to savory donut-like fritters made with gram flour. In Rajasthan, they are added to a thick chickpea stew. The leaves are also contained in the curry pastes of Madras and Sri Lanka.

✤ HEALING POWER

Helps with digestion, blood sugar regulation, and skin infection. Also reduces congestion, and protects the liver.

WHERE TO BUY IT: Indian market, online. May be labeled "meetha neem" or "kari patta." Or grow your own in a pot near a window.

HOW TO STORE IT: Best when fresh—they will keep for a week. Dried leaves are flavorless, but fresh leaves can be frozen.

COMPLEMENTS

cauliflower
coconut milk
eggplant
lentils

onions
potatoes
seafood
tomatoes

PAIRS WELL WITH

cilantro
cinnamon
cloves
coriander
cumin
fennel
fenugreek
garlic
mustard seeds
tamarind
turmeric

FLAVOR PROFILE: *spicy curry flavor with notes of pine and citrus*

Coconut Chutney

Prep time: 30 minutes

Makes about 1 cup *Use this spicy South Indian coconut chutney alongside curries, soups, Indian dosas (fermented crepes made from rice batter and black lentils), or even on pancakes. If you have a readily available supply of fresh coconuts, consider doubling the recipe—this chutney goes fast.*

2 cups coconut meat (from one fresh coconut)
3 fresh green chiles
1½ teaspoons fresh minced ginger
Salt
8 ounces coconut water
5 curry leaves
1 tablespoon coconut oil or cooking oil
2 whole red chiles
1 teaspoon mustard seeds

Remove the skin from the coconut and grate it.

Slit and seed the green chiles.

In a blender or food processor, mix the green chiles, ginger, salt, grated coconut, and coconut water until a fine paste forms.

Transfer the paste to a small glass bowl or container, and add the curry leaves.

In a large pan over medium heat, heat the coconut oil. Add the red chiles and stir for a few seconds.

Add the mustard seeds and fry until they start to pop.

Pour the chili oil into the paste and mix.

Refrigerate.

Prep time: 1 hour | Cook time: 30 minutes

Serves 4 *This spice-rich curry from South India contains 20 curry leaves and is delicious over rice with yogurt. Traditionally, this curry is eaten off a plate made from banana leaves while sitting on the floor. Try it also with Coconut Chutney (here).*

1⅔ pounds fresh mushrooms
⅔ cup coconut oil or ghee, divided
¾ cup grated coconut
¼ cup raw cashews
¼ cup coconut water
2 teaspoons cumin seeds
1 teaspoon mustard seeds
1 cup chopped onion
4 teaspoons minced fresh ginger
4 teaspoons minced fresh garlic
2 teaspoons ground coriander
1 teaspoon ground cayenne pepper
1 teaspoon ground turmeric
Salt
1 cup chopped tomatoes
20 curry leaves
1⅔ pounds fresh or frozen peas

Using a wet paper towel, clean the mushrooms. Slice them.

In a large pan over medium heat, cook the mushrooms with 3 tablespoons of oil for 5 minutes.

In a blender, mix the coconut, cashews, and coconut water to make a paste.

Heat the remaining roughly ½ cup of oil in a large saucepan. Add the cumin seeds and mustard seeds, and sauté until the mustard seeds pop.

Add the onion and sauté until golden; then add the ginger and garlic and stir.

Add the coriander, cayenne, and turmeric, season with salt, and stir.

Add the tomatoes, reduce the heat to low, and add the coconut paste and curry leaves. Stir, adding approximately 2 cups water.

Bring to a boil and add the peas and mushrooms.

Simmer for 5 minutes and add more salt if needed.

Serve over rice.

Fenugreek

Fenugreek, also known as Greek hay, is native to the Mediterranean, Southern Europe, the Caucasus, and West Asia. Remains of fenugreek found in Iraq date its usage back to 4,000 years ago, when ancient Egyptians used it as incense to embalm the dead. In North Africa the ground seeds were mixed with olive oil and sugar for weight gain. Some women celebrated it for its ability to increase breast size, while lactation consultant Kathleen Huggins has witnessed that almost all mothers taking capsules of the herb have been able to increase their milk supply. To repel invaders during the first Jewish/Roman war in Jerusalem, Jewish soldiers poured over the city walls boiling oil mixed with fenugreek, a concoction that resembled boiling buckets of okra. Fenugreek contains mucilage, a glutinous substance that may also prevent absorption of prescription drugs. Now New Jersey has its own plant for processing fenugreek for use in perfumes and the flavoring agents of imitation maple syrup, butterscotch, and vanilla.

In the Kitchen *The seeds are roasted before use because the raw seeds are bitter, but long cooking time will mellow the flavor. The seeds are very hard, and a mortar and pestle is the best way to grind them. Roasted seeds can also be used as a coffee substitute. Alternatively, the seeds can be sprouted and added to salad. The fresh leaves can be strewn over the top of a salad or herb omelet as well. Apart from the unique flavor and aroma, fenugreek seeds can also contribute a thick, slippery texture to dishes. Or a pinch can be sprinkled over yogurt and cooked greens.*

✳ REGIONAL STAR

Fenugreek is used in pickles, dals, and the sambar powder of India. Fresh fenugreek leaves, called *methi*, are also added to potatoes, breads, spinach, rice, and fish curries. Fenugreek is one of the essential spices in the Georgian spice mixture *khmeli suneli*. And fresh or dried, they are equally great in Iranian lamb stew.

✚ HEALING POWER

High in vitamins, minerals, and protein, fenugreek also aids in digestive disorders such as constipation, loss of appetite, gastritis, lowering blood sugar, bronchitis, and chapped lips. Women use it while breastfeeding to promote milk flow. It can also be used as a poultice for inflammation and gout. Fenugreek is additionally thought to be an aphrodisiac, laxative, and astringent. Like turmeric, fenugreek is an anti-inflammatory, and a teaspoon of fenugreek seeds a day can help with arthritis and joint pain.

WHERE TO BUY IT: specialty spice shops for dried fenugreek. Look for the leaves at Middle Eastern markets. If you have a garden with full sun, you can grow it yourself and make use of the leaves as well as the seeds.

HOW TO STORE IT: Fresh leaves last in the refrigerator for 2 to 3 days. Ground fenugreek loses its flavor rapidly, so store it away from moisture, and only grind when needed.

chickpeas
mashed potatoes
mung beans and other daals
paneer cheese
turnips
vegetables
walnuts
yogurt

PAIRS WELL WITH

cardamom
cilantro
cinnamon
cloves
cumin
fennel
garlic
mustard
turmeric

FLAVOR PROFILE: *maple syrup aroma but a more bitter taste, like burnt sugar*

Fenugreek Pumpkin

Prep time: 5 minutes | Cook time: 5 to 7 minutes

Serves 2 *This is a simple dish prepared in an Indian style that balances the flavors of spicy, bitter, salty, sour and sweet, while making use of fenugreek's healing properties.*

3 tablespoons coconut oil, ghee, or other cooking oil
2 teaspoons mustard seeds
2 teaspoons ground fenugreek
1 teaspoon ground cumin
1 teaspoon ground turmeric
2 cups chopped fresh pumpkin
1 teaspoon peeled and grated fresh ginger
Fenugreek leaves (optional)
1 tablespoon brown sugar, or Indian *jaggery*
Juice of 1 lemon, or 1 tablespoon tamarind
Salt
Freshly ground black pepper

In a large pan over medium-high heat, heat the coconut oil. Add the mustard seeds and sauté until they begin to pop, about 2 minutes.

Add the fenugreek and stir until it slightly browns, about 5 minutes.

Add the cumin, turmeric, pumpkin, ginger, and fenugreek leaves (if using), and stir.

Add the brown sugar and lemon juice, and season with salt and pepper.

Serve.

Eggplant with Fenugreek Yogurt Sauce

Prep time: 15 minutes | Cook time: 30 minutes

Serves 2 *This dish is adapted from a recipe that originally used saffron and pine nuts. This version replaces those with fenugreek and walnuts for a twist. Both versions are equally delicious.*

2 small eggplants
2 tablespoons extra-virgin olive oil
Salt
Freshly ground black pepper
¼ cup finely chopped walnuts
½ cup Greek yogurt
2 tablespoons freshly squeezed lemon juice
½ teaspoon roasted and ground fenugreek
4 basil sprigs, torn
Seeds of 1 pomegranate

Preheat the oven to 425°F.

Halve the eggplants, drizzle them with the olive oil, and season with salt and pepper.

Bake for 20 to 30 minutes, until tender and lightly brown.

While the eggplants are cooking, in a large pan over medium-high heat, roast the walnuts for a few minutes, until they develop a roasted smell, being careful not to let them get too dark. (It happens quickly.) Set them aside to cool.

In a small bowl, stir together the yogurt, lemon juice, and fenugreek, and season with salt and pepper.

When the eggplants are done, allow them to cool slightly.

Top with the yogurt sauce, basil, toasted walnuts, and pomegranate seeds, and serve.

TIP: Removing the seeds from a pomegranate can be a chore. Many pomegranate fans recommend cutting it into sections and taking the seeds out in a bowl of water. An even quicker way is this: Hold the pomegranate in your hand, stem-side down. Using a knife, cut all around the center of the pomegranate as if you were cutting it in half, but only cut through the peel. Break the fruit open into two halves, pushing up from the back of it to loosen it. Hold the pomegranate in your palm, seed-side down, over a bowl. With a wooden spoon, continuously whack the back of the pomegranate. All the seeds should fall out.

Ginger

First cultivated in China, ginger has been used by humans for more than 3,000 years. Although it's not yet supported by medical science, the American Cancer Society advises consuming ginger regularly to ward off the growth of tumors. Ginger contains the compound gingerol, which has sedative and antibacterial properties and can inhibit ovarian cancer cells. The most common medicinal uses of ginger, however, are to settle an upset stomach, prevent motion sickness, and help with morning sickness. Since eating it makes you sweat, it can also break a fever. In Chinese medicine, it's believed to be a libido booster and aphrodisiac. In the Middle Ages, it could be found on the table as commonly as salt.

In the Kitchen *Fresh ginger has a decidedly different flavor and texture from the dried and ground ginger more commonly used in baking. Use fresh ginger in savory dishes, especially those from Asia. Whole, unpeeled pieces can be added to savory stews for extra flavor and then removed before serving or added to stir-fried greens like bok choy. Grating or mashing up ginger in a food processor and then squeezing it through a cheesecloth will produce a juice you can either add to marinades or use to make an invigorating tonic with lemon or lime and honey. These days ginger is a common flavoring additive to the fermented beverage kombucha.*

REGIONAL STAR

Originally grown in China, the ginger root is now used in almost all regional cuisines of the world, especially in the form of a tonic. Almost every country has some form of ginger ale, beer, wine, or tea. On the Ivory Coast, a drink is made from fresh ginger, lemon, orange, and pineapple, and France makes a ginger-flavored liquor called Canton. It's also consumed in candied or pickled form to aid digestion. Koreans use it extensively in the preparation of kimchi, while throughout the West, it's used as a pickling spice.

HEALING POWER

A teaspoon of fresh grated ginger in a glass of boiling water, cooled and then drunk, is the most reliable cure for an upset stomach. Ginger is also an anti-inflammatory and a warming spice.

WHERE TO BUY IT: supermarket, Asian market

HOW TO STORE IT: Fresh ginger can last in the refrigerator for about 10 days. Stored in syrup or dried, it can last for 2 years.

COMPLEMENTS

bananas
broccoli
cashews
chocolate

figs
grapefruit
green beans
lemon
lime
peanut sauces
tahini salad dressings

PAIRS WELL WITH

---

basil
cilantro
garlic
lemongrass
mint
onion
soy sauce

FLAVOR PROFILE: *Fresh: hot and tangy, warm with an earthy, woody scent. Younger roots are milder than mature ones. Dry: bittersweet and spicy*

Prep time: 10 minutes | Cook time: 10 minutes

Serves 2 to 4 *Some cooks keep little bowls of freshly grated ginger and garlic next to the stove so they can throw some into every dish. This recipe combines ginger and garlic with a little lemon and soy sauce to make a simple but satisfying vegetarian meal served over rice. If you like, add cubes of firm tofu for a boost of protein or cashews on top for a garnish.*

2 garlic cloves, crushed
2 teaspoons peeled and minced fresh ginger root
4 tablespoons coconut or vegetable oil, divided
2 tablespoons soy sauce
Juice of ½ lemon, plus more for serving
1 head broccoli or cauliflower
¾ cup julienned carrots (sliced into matchsticks)
½ cup green beans or snow peas
½ onion, chopped
Salt
Freshly ground black pepper
Cashews (optional)

In a large bowl, toss together the garlic, ginger, 2 tablespoons of coconut oil, the soy sauce, lemon juice, broccoli, carrots, green beans, and onion.

In a large frying pan over medium heat, heat the remaining 2 tablespoons of coconut oil.

Add the vegetable mixture and sauté for a few minutes, until cooked but still crisp.

Squeeze the additional lemon juice on top, season with salt and pepper, and add cashews (if using).

Serve immediately over rice.

TIP: If you are using cashews and want them to stay crunchy, add them at the end of cooking. If you have never tried cooking with brewer's yeast, it is available at most health food stores. It adds a unique flavor and creamy sauce to your vegetables. Try substituting 1 tablespoon brewer's yeast and a few tablespoons of water for the soy sauce.

Prep time: 1 minute | Cook time: 5 minutes

Serves 1 *This chai actually tastes how it is served at Indian restaurants: sweet and creamy with spicy, sweet notes—not the type of chai you typically find at Starbucks. If you have leftover chai, try substituting it for water or milk when cooking oatmeal.*

½ cup water
½ teaspoon fresh ginger or ¼ teaspoon ground
½ teaspoon black tea (For traditional Indian chai, try using "mamri" tea, which is in granules instead of leaves. If using regular tea leaves, increase measurement to 1 teaspoon. If using tea bags, use 2.)
½ cup milk
⅛ teaspoon ground cinnamon
Pinch pepper
⅛ teaspoon ground cardamom
Sugar (optional)

In a small pot over high heat, bring the water and fresh ginger to a boil.

Add the black tea, milk, cinnamon, pepper, and cardamom.

Let it boil till it becomes the color of caramel, about 5 minutes.

Add sugar (if using). Stir and pour.

TIP: For an even creamier version, add less water and more milk. Sugar can be added earlier, but make sure to stir; otherwise, it sits at the bottom and burns, giving a caramel flavor to the tea. Cardamom is a very volatile spice, so it should be added near the end if using powder; otherwise, it tends to evaporate. Black pepper and ginger are both great for sore throats, so increase those if you have a cold. Lemongrass, fresh mint, or tulsi (Indian basil) can be added to the tea as well.

Juniper Berry

Juniper berries are the only spice from the cypress family. The berries take two to three years to ripen, so if you find them in the wild, only pick the blue ones. Native to Europe, they grow profusely all over North America, though the berries are mealier, and less tasty, than the European variety. The word *gin* is actually derived from the word *juniper*, and the Dutch have used the unripe green berries for flavoring gin since the seventeenth century. Since juniper berries are peppery, Romans used them as a cheap substitute for the black pepper they were importing from India. According to the folklore surrounding the juniper berry, if you burn the branches, you can purify the air, and if you put a juniper branch in front of your door, the only way a witch can get past it is by counting all the needles. Juniper berries have also been known to make urine smell like violets.

In the Kitchen *The volatile oils are strongest when the juniper berry is used fresh; once dried, the flavor diminishes. Crush them in a mortar and pestle with salt and garlic, and add the mixture to a marinade for lamb or pork. You'll only need about four or five to flavor the dish without overpowering it. Juniper berries are also good for gamey meats, so get out your juniper berries next time you plan to marinate a blackbird, thrush, woodcock, or a wild boar. Juniper berries can be added to casseroles, pickles, root vegetables, and even fruitcake.*

❋ REGIONAL STAR

Scandinavians use juniper berries extensively in marinades for beef and pork, and the Finns also make a rye beer with them. In Belgium, kidneys are marinated with them, and the French use them for venison, while Germany, Austria, Poland, and Hungary use them in sauerkrauts and roasts. Hungary is the primary cultivator of juniper berries, though, arguably, the tastiest ones come from Macedonia and Albania.

✚ HEALING POWER

The berries have been used as both an appetite suppressant and appetite stimulant.

WHERE TO BUY IT: Most specialty grocery stores online, or buy them whole and plant a juniper bush

HOW TO STORE IT: When the seeds dry out, they lose their flavor. Fresh berries last about six months.

COMPLEMENTS

apple
artichokes
cabbage

duck
gin
goose
marinades
olive oil
pickles
potato
quail
rice
root vegetables
sauerkraut
vinegar

PAIRS WELL WITH

bay leaf
black pepper
caraway seeds
coriander seed
fennel
garlic
rosemary
thyme

FLAVOR PROFILE: *bitter-sour with notes of citrus, pine resin, and gin*

Juniper Berry Brine

Prep time: 5 minutes | Cook time: 30 minutes

Serves 20 *This recipe is from Julio Mis, sous chef at Sociale in San Francisco. This recipe makes enough brine for about 20 Cornish game hens. You can cut the recipe in half, but Julio advises making the brine in large batches and freezing it until needed, because it's great to have a brine on hand for general cooking purposes. This brine also works well for pork, chicken, turkey, and rabbit.*

**1½ cups white sugar
¾ cup kosher salt
¼ cup juniper berries
¼ cup star anise
⅓ cup coriander seed
2 tablespoons fennel seed
2 tablespoons black peppercorns
1 tablespoon whole cloves
15 whole garlic cloves
20 broken bay leaves
Zest of 4 lemons**

In a large pot over medium-low heat, simmer the sugar, salt, juniper berries, star anise, coriander, fennel seed, peppercorns, cloves, garlic, bay leaves, and lemon zest in 8 quarts of water for 30 minutes.

Allow the brine to cool completely before adding meat to it.

TIP: Soaking meat in brine for 1 to 4 hours ensures that it will be moist after it's cooked. After brining, grill or bake as desired.

Juniper Berry Simple Syrup

Prep time: 1 minute | Cook time: 2 minutes

Makes 1 cup *Use this syrup to make cocktails or lemonade. To make candied juniper berries, lavender, or rosemary flowers, boil the berries or flowers in the sugar syrup for about 5 minutes. Remove them from the syrup and set them on a plate. A clear glaze of sugar will cover them beautifully.*

- **1 cup granulated sugar**
- **1 cup water**
- **4 tablespoons juniper berries**
- **3 sprigs rosemary or lavender (optional)**

In a small pot over medium heat, stir the sugar into the water until the sugar has dissolved.

Add the juniper berries and rosemary (if using), and stir until the mixture begins to boil. Do not let the syrup boil too long, or it will get too thick when it cools.

Remove from the heat and allow the syrup to cool.

Transfer the syrup to a mason jar or other container with a lid, and keep in the refrigerator for up to a month.

TIP: For a lemon-gin-juniper cocktail, combine 1 ounce gin, 1 ounce freshly squeezed lemon juice, and 1 tablespoon juniper simple syrup in a shaker filled with ice. Shake, pour into a champagne flute, and top with champagne.

Mace

The spice mace has nothing to do with the commonly known pepper spray, which should not be used in cooking! Mace comes from the outer yellow sheath of the nutmeg seed of the Myristica tree, and harvesting the seed requires a seven-year wait. The flavor of the spice resembles a cross between nutmeg and black pepper. Originally grown on the Banda Islands of Indonesia, it's now also grown in Granada. One of the trendiest spices of the eighteenth century, when it was fashionably paired with apples, mace has been nearly forgotten today. Although mace and nutmeg are sisters from the same tree, like some sisters, they also compete; therefore, it's best to use them separately. Nutmeg is more commonly used in cooking because it contains 10 times the yield of mace and is therefore a better value. Like nutmeg, mace contains eugenol, which can aid sleep, cure digestive disorders, relieve toothaches, and is even used in some skin creams to alleviate acne and tired joints.

In the Kitchen *Similar to nutmeg, but with a less sweet, more delicate flavor, mace can be used for its saffron-like qualities or substituted for nutmeg. In flavor, ¼ teaspoon of mace is equal to ¼ teaspoon of nutmeg. Because of its potency, you usually don't want to use more than ¼ teaspoon of either spice in a recipe. Try it on sweet potatoes, pumpkins, or puréed carrots; rhubarb or cherry pie; or custards, puddings, or donuts. Or for breakfast, mace can be added to eggs or lightly sprinkled over oatmeal. When possible, mace should be added toward the end of cooking, since it can become slightly bitter when cooked.*

REGIONAL STAR

In European cuisine, mace is used to flavor potatoes and meat and can be added with onion to creamy béchamel sauces, fish stocks, desserts, and cheese soufflés. It's also used in spinach, lamb, and cabbage dishes and in pickles. In Southeast Asia and China, mace is considered a medicine more than a food.

HEALING POWER

acts as an anti-inflammatory, lowers blood sugar and cholesterol, helps prevent tooth decay, fights cancer, enhances mood

WHERE TO BUY IT: supermarket, specialty grocery store, online

HOW TO STORE IT: Mace retains its flavor longer than other spices when stored. The more orange the color, the higher its quality.

COMPLEMENTS

apples
baked goods
cherries
chocolate
cranberries

custards
donuts
eggs
maple syrup
potatoes
pumpkin
raisins
rhubarb
sauces
stuffings
veal
yams

PAIRS WELL WITH

allspice
cinnamon
cloves
cumin
ginger
vanilla

FLAVOR PROFILE: *sweet, warm, and spicy*

Prep time: 20 to 30 minutes, plus 1 hour to chill dough | Cook time: 20 minutes

Makes 12 cookies *When Russians talk about politics, they call them* pryaniki, *as in spicy as their gingerbread cookies. These cookies, however, spread with a layer of plum jam and flavored with mace, definitely taste better than politics.*

2 tablespoons butter, at room temperature
½ cup honey (clover is best)
1 egg
1¾ cups flour
½ teaspoon baking soda
¼ teaspoon ground cardamom
¼ teaspoon ground ginger
½ teaspoon ground mace
½ teaspoon ground cinnamon
2 tablespoons crushed almonds
½ cup thick plum jam
½ cup confectioners' sugar
2 tablespoons freshly squeezed lemon juice

In a small bowl, blend together the butter and honey.

Beat in the egg.

Stir in the flour, baking soda, cardamom, ginger, mace, cinnamon, and almonds.

Wrap the dough in waxed paper or aluminum foil and refrigerate it for an hour.

Preheat the oven to 350°F.

On a floured board, using a rolling pin, roll the dough out into ⅛-inch thickness.

Cut out rounds with a 2½-inch cookie cutter.

Spread a teaspoon of jam onto one round and top with a plain round, sealing them by crimping the edges so all the jam is inside. Repeat to make the remaining cookies.

Place each cookie on a greased baking sheet and bake for 15 to 20 minutes.

Let the cookies cool on the rack.

In a small bowl, mix together the confectioners' sugar and lemon juice.

Pour the lemon-sugar mixture over the cooled cookies, and serve with tea.

TIP: If you don't have a round cookie cutter, you can also use a heart or other-shaped one, or even a knife to cut out a circle. For bigger cookies, use the lid of a mason jar. When rolling the dough, make sure the surface of the board, as well as the rolling pin, is covered with flour.

Prep time: 20 minutes | Cook time: 35 minutes

Serves 4 *Mace brings out the sweetness of the carrots in this recipe. For an even sweeter variation, substitute half the carrots for sweet potato or winter squash. For an additional treat, top with toasted pumpkin seeds or poppy seeds.*

2 tablespoons butter
1 yellow onion, chopped
1 teaspoon salt, plus more for seasoning
½ teaspoon ground mace
½ teaspoon ground turmeric
½ teaspoon ground ginger
4 cups chicken stock
1 pound carrots, peeled and chopped into 1-inch chunks
Freshly ground black pepper
½ cup toasted pumpkin seeds or poppy seeds (optional)

In a large pot over medium heat, melt the butter.

Add the onion and stir until soft and translucent, about 10 minutes.

Add the salt, mace, turmeric, and ginger, and cook for another 2 minutes.

Add the chicken stock and carrots, and cover.

Simmer over low heat for about 25 minutes, until the carrots are tender.

Cool the soup slightly, transfer to a blender or use a stick blender, and purée.

Season with salt and pepper.

Serve topped with the toasted pumpkin seeds (if using).

Mustard

Mustard is one of those spices that truly illustrate how the cuisines of a region are spawned by the foods produced there. The word for mustard comes from the phrase "burning wine" in Latin, referring to how the seeds were cracked like black pepper on the plate and mixed with wine to create a condiment. Related to Brussels sprouts, collard, and kale, 40 varieties of mustard produce either black, white, or yellow seeds. Today, in many parts of the United States, mustard flowers blaze up in the spring—and most people don't realize that you can eat these zesty flowers, too. One of the few spices cultivated in the Northern Hemisphere, mustard was the principal spice before the spice trade commenced. In the medieval period, it was the one spice common people could actually afford. According to Marie Nadine Antol in her guide to the lore and quint-essential history of mustard, guests at one fourteenth-century event consumed over 70 pounds of mustard cream!

In the Kitchen *To make refined mustard powder, the husk is removed and the seeds are finely ground. Powdered mustard works well in barbecue sauces, salad dressings, cream sauces, and mac and cheese. Young mustard leaves are bitter but tasty and can be eaten in salads; when the leaves become more mature, they can be stir-fried. The pungency of the mustard seed is not activated until it is cracked and mixed with a liquid. The type of liquid it's mixed with determines the flavor: Vinegar provides a mild zing while beer heats it up. Water gives it the most heat of all, but you'll get more blaze with cold water than hot.*

❋ REGIONAL STAR

In India, black mustard seeds are fried in ghee until they pop, and then other spices and vegetables are added to the mixture. Raw mustard seeds are ground to make paste for curries. In Vietnam, mustard leaves are used as a wrap. Prepared mustards range from mild French mustards to the Bavarian mustards of Germany.

✚ HEALING POWER

Rich in magnesium and selenium, mustard seed is helpful in reducing the severity of arthritis. Mustard seed oil has been used to stimulate hair growth. Added to massage oils, it helps with arthritis and inflammation. In Ayurveda, mustard is a warming oil consumed during the cold months. One teaspoon of mustard seeds two to three times a day can also help relieve constipation.

WHERE TO BUY IT: White mustard seeds are easier to find than black ones. Prepared mustard seeds are available in supermarkets, specialty grocery stores, and online.

HOW TO STORE IT: When dry, mustard powder and seeds last a long time. Prepared mustard can be stored at room temperature for a few months, even after opening.

COMPLEMENTS

arugula
cabbage
capers
cheeses
cream sauces
glazes with brown sugar
ham
mayonnaise
meats
pecans
salad dressings
sausages
smoked fish
soy sauce
vinegar
wine

PAIRS WELL WITH

bay leaf
dill
fennel
honey
tarragon

FLAVOR PROFILE: *ranges from hot to bitter to sweet*

Sautéed Kale with Mustard Seeds

Prep time: 5 minutes | Cook time: 10 minutes

Serves 2 or 3 *If you love the bitter, spicy taste of mustard greens but can't find them anywhere, here's an easy way to achieve that flavor using kale instead. This dish also demonstrates how naturally mustard pairs with white wine vinegar.*

2 tablespoons extra-virgin olive oil or coconut oil
1 tablespoon whole mustard seeds
1 large bunch kale, washed, stemmed, and cut into 1-inch strips
Salt
Freshly ground black pepper
2 tablespoons white wine vinegar

In a large nonstick pan over medium heat, heat the olive oil.

Add the mustard seeds and sauté until they begin to pop, about 2 minutes.

Add the kale and stir the leaves to coat them with the oil and mustard seeds.

Season with salt and pepper and continue to stir for a few more minutes, until the leaves are slightly wilted and tender. They will cook down considerably.

Add the white wine vinegar and serve immediately.

TIP: You can use chard or any other greens to make this dish. One of the first steps in some Indian dishes is to heat the oil, and then add mustard seeds until they pop. This flavors the oil. Indian dishes often involve many complicated procedures after that, but this recipe keeps the dish simple. If the mustard seeds don't pop, don't worry. They will start to pop after you add the greens. You can also add a few chopped shallots to this dish, if desired.

Roasted Pork Chops with Basil-Mustard Sauce

Prep time: 5 minutes | Cook time: 10 minutes

Serves 2 *These pork chops are baked in the oven at a high heat. The sauce, which uses prepared Dijon mustard, is spooned onto the pork when serving. This simple sauce is delicious with lamb as well. Serve this dish with bitter greens and a baked potato.*

½ bunch fresh basil, stemmed
2 garlic cloves
2 tablespoons Dijon mustard
3 tablespoons extra-virgin olive oil, divided
Salt
Freshly ground black pepper
2 pork chops

In a blender, blend the basil, garlic, mustard, and 2 tablespoons of olive oil until smooth.

Season with salt and pepper.

According to your preference, you may want to add more mustard or basil. Set aside.

Set the oven rack at the lowest position.

Preheat the oven to 500°F.

Heat an ovenproof skillet over high heat for a few minutes, until it is extremely hot. Be sure to use oven mitts when handling it.

Meanwhile, rub the pork chops with the remaining 1 tablespoon of olive oil.

121

Add the chops to the hot skillet and transfer to the oven.

Cook for 5 minutes on each side.

Serve with the basil-mustard sauce on top.

TIP: An alternate cooking method is to panfry pork chops over the stove and sear in the juices using the following method: Salt and pepper the chops. Heat a pan over medium-high heat for a few minutes; then add 2 tablespoons of olive or cooking oil. When the oil is hot, add the chops and cook them on high for 2 minutes on each side, until brown. Reduce the heat and add ½ cup wine, stock, or other liquid. Cook on high for 3 minutes, until the liquid has almost evaporated; then turn the heat to low, cover, and cook for an additional 10 to 15 minutes. Add lemon, parsley, basil-mustard sauce, or any other condiment.

Nutmeg

Nutmeg isn't actually a nut, so those with nut allergies need not be concerned. It's the seed of an evergreen tree grown in the Banda Islands of Indonesia, the only tree that produces two spices, the other being mace, the outer reddish covering of the seed. The culinary historian Michael Krondl suggests nutmeg was the iPhone of the 1600s because of its enormous popularity and range of potential. All the rage with the beau monde, nutmeg was not only used in the kitchen but could also fight the Black Plague and induce both abortions and menstruation. Perhaps another reason for its popularity was that nutmeg contains myristicin, a substance that can produce a sort of hazy, unpleasant hallucination with side effects so dire that it never caught on as a drug. According to nutmeg lore, the Dutch traded Manhattan for nutmeg. Well, not exactly. The British wanted control of New York, and the Dutch wanted that last nutmeg-producing island in Indonesia, so they made a deal.

In the Kitchen *Since nutmeg loses its flavor so quickly, it's best to buy it whole and get a nutmeg grater so you can impress your friends by grating it over glasses of cold eggnog or a Ramos fizz. Its aroma will fill your kitchen, though ingesting too much of it, combined with alcohol, can induce its hallucinogenic properties. Like mace (but cheaper), nutmeg can be added to hot chocolate, hot cereal, apples, custards, puddings, cakes, fruit pastries, bananas, and pumpkin pies. It can also be used in savory dishes.*

⁛ REGIONAL STAR

Arabic countries use nutmeg in lamb dishes and in the Moroccan spice blend *ras el hanout*. The French use nutmeg in soups and stews, and the Dutch add it to vegetables like cauliflower and cabbage. In most Asian countries it is primarily used medicinally.

✚ HEALING POWER

Helps with sleep as well as muscular and joint pain. Use in moderation, as more than a tablespoon of nutmeg can cause extremely unpleasant side effects.

WHERE TO BUY IT: supermarket, specialty grocery store, online

HOW TO STORE IT: Whole seeds are best since the aroma is lost soon after grinding.

COMPLEMENTS

acorn squash
apples
baked goods
bananas
chowders
cream sauces
egg dishes

**lamb
mushrooms
noodles
pumpkin
spinach
stewed fruit**

**allspice
cardamom
cinnamon
cloves
ginger**

FLAVOR PROFILE: *sweet, warm, and woodsy*

Prep time: 5 minutes | Cook time: 10 minutes

Serves 2 or 3 *The combination of parsley, garlic, nutmeg, and cream makes for a delicious but simple meal. For a spicier version, add ¼ to ½ teaspoon cayenne pepper.*

½ cup extra-virgin olive oil
½ cup chopped Italian parsley
3 large garlic cloves, minced
12 ounces spaghetti
2 tomatoes, chopped
3 tablespoons cream
½ teaspoon freshly grated nutmeg
Salt
Freshly ground black pepper
Parmesan cheese, for garnish
¼ cup toasted walnuts, finely chopped

In a small bowl, mix the olive oil, parsley, and garlic. Set aside.

In a large pot over high heat, boil the pasta in the amount of water and for the time indicated by the package directions, until cooked (tender but not too soft).

Drain the spaghetti and return the pasta to the pot.

Add the oil mixture, tomatoes, cream, and nutmeg, and season with salt and pepper.

Sprinkle with Parmesan cheese and toasted walnuts, and serve.

TIP: The classic French blend called *quatre épices*, or "four spices," is usually used to glaze ham or add to pâté, but to experience the flavor that dominated early European food, substitute 1 teaspoon of this blend for the nutmeg. To make it, grind together 1 tablespoon black peppercorns, 1 teaspoon grated nutmeg, ½ teaspoon cloves, and ½ teaspoon ginger.

Creamy Spinach Soup with Nutmeg

Prep time: 15 minutes | Cook time: 30 minutes

Serves 4 *Spinach and nutmeg make a perfect pair in this deliciously warming soup. For a less rich soup, decrease the amount of cream, or just drizzle it on top of individual servings. Serve with hot bread for a simple yet satisfying meal.*

2 tablespoons butter
1 small onion, finely chopped
1 small shallot, minced
2 garlic cloves, minced
4 cups chicken stock
4 cups spinach
Zest of ½ lemon
½ cup heavy cream
Salt
Freshly grated black pepper
Freshly grated nutmeg, for garnish

In a large saucepan over medium heat, melt the butter.

Add the onion and shallot, and sauté until softened.

Add the garlic and cook for another minute.

Add the stock and simmer for about 10 minutes.

Add the spinach and continue to simmer for about 5 minutes, until the spinach is wilted.

Using a food processor, blender, or stick blender, blend the soup into a smooth purée. You may have to do this in 2 batches.

Return the soup to the saucepan.

Add the lemon zest and cream, and reheat. Season with salt and pepper, and garnish with nutmeg.

Serve immediately.

TIP: For an alternative version, try substituting steamed broccoli for the spinach.

Paprika

During autumn in Eastern Europe and the Balkans, strings of paprika peppers hang on fences, and the streets are redolent with the aroma of roasting peppers. Throughout this region, a paprika shaker on the table replaces black pepper. Hungary appropriated this "red gold" as its own national spice, but this red pepper, like all red peppers, actually came from Southern Mexico and Central America when Columbus set out to find black pepper and returned with a paprika plant. The chemical capsaicin, found in chile peppers (different from the piperine in black pepper), is the active agent that produces the sensation of heat. The *Capsicum annuum* family of peppers includes sweet bell peppers, hot green peppers, and hot red peppers. Any combination of these can be dried and made into paprika, which is why the colors and flavors vary. They range in flavor from the sweet Hungarian to the smoky Spanish to the fiery hot. Paprika peppers have seven times as much vitamin C as oranges.

In the Kitchen *When unheated, paprika's flavor remains mild, so it can be added for its color at the end of cooking or used on cold dishes, as it is commonly seen dusted on top of deviled eggs or potato salads. But paprika can be used for much more. To increase paprika's flavor, sauté it in a little oil before adding it to your dish. When you use it in a rub for chicken or fish, remember that its high sugar content means it can burn easily. Paprika pairs well with chicken, fish, rice, pasta with tomato or cream sauces, and cauliflower. Add it to cottage cheese or sour cream, or sprinkle it on French-fried potatoes.*

❋ REGIONAL STAR

Hungarian and Eastern European cuisines use the hotter variety of paprika to make goulash and chicken paprika. Portugal and Morocco use the Spanish variety, which gets its smoky flavor from being smoked over oak fires. Paprika is generally added to tandoori chicken in Indian cuisine, giving it its characteristic red color.

✚ HEALING POWER

rich in vitamins A, B_6, C, and E. The chemical capsaicin relaxes blood vessels, which is known to decrease blood pressure. Applied as a topical cream, it can relieve pain. Ingested, the heating agents make you sweat and release endorphins.

WHERE TO BUY IT: supermarket, or for more varieties, a specialty grocery store or online

HOW TO STORE IT: Paprika is semiperishable, lasting about four months, and should be stored in a cool, dry place such as a pantry.

COMPLEMENTS

beef
chicken

131

chickpeas
duck
eggplant
mushrooms
onion
pasta
rice
roasted vegetables
sour cream
tahini
veal
white cheeses
yogurt

PAIRS WELL WITH

garlic
ginger
oregano
parsley
saffron
turmeric

FLAVOR PROFILE: *sweet to smoky to spicy to slightly bitter-sour.*

Matt's Paprika Rub for Ribs or Pulled Pork

Prep time: 5 minutes, plus 2 to 24 hours to marinate | Cook time: 2 hours for ribs, 6 hours for pork

Serves 4 *Banker by day, rib cook-off champion by weekend, Matt Elliott provides this recipe for his favorite rib rub or pulled pork. To finish it, he adds a bottle of barbecue sauce. You can make your own, or as Matt recommends, "Buy whatever is on sale." This dry rub will make enough to cover either a pork shoulder to make pulled pork or a beef rack of ribs.*

FOR THE PAPRIKA RUB
½ cup brown sugar
⅓ cup mixed dried herbs: rosemary, thyme, oregano
¼ cup salt
¼ cup ground paprika
3 tablespoons ground cayenne pepper
Handful of fresh herbs: rosemary, thyme, oregano

FOR THE BEEF RACK OF RIBS
Beef rack of ribs
1 (18-ounce) bottle barbecue sauce

FOR THE PULLED PORK
Pork shoulder
1 cup chicken or beef stock
1 (18-ounce) bottle barbecue sauce

TO MAKE THE PAPRIKA RUB
In a small bowl, mix together the brown sugar, dried herbs, salt, paprika, cayenne pepper, and fresh herbs.

TO MAKE THE BEEF RACK OF RIBS

Preheat the oven to 250°F.

Slather the paprika rub over the ribs.

Wrap the ribs in foil and bake for 2 hours.

Remove the ribs from the oven and set the oven to broil.

Pour the barbecue sauce over the ribs and broil them until evenly browned and the sauce is bubbling, about 5 minutes.

Serve.

TO MAKE THE PULLED PORK

Slather the paprika rub over the pork and marinate it for 2 hours to overnight.

Put it in a slow cooker on high and cook for 6 hours with the chicken stock.

Remove the bone and chop up the meat.

Pour the barbecue sauce over the meat, mix, and serve.

Brown Rice or Noodles with Mushroom-Paprika Cream Sauce

Prep time: 5 minutes | Cook time: 15 minutes

Serves 2 *This sauce was originally designed to be poured over fish. Combined with mushrooms, it works really well over pasta and is reminiscent of goulash. For a gluten-free meal, try it over rice.*

1 cup mushrooms, sliced
5 tablespoons butter, divided
2 tablespoons all-purpose flour
½ teaspoon salt
½ teaspoon freshly ground black pepper
1 cup whole milk or cream
½ teaspoon minced garlic
1 teaspoon minced onion
3 teaspoons ground Hungarian paprika
Pinch ground nutmeg
Dash white wine (if desired)

In a medium saucepan over medium heat, sauté the mushrooms in 1 tablespoon of butter until they are golden, about 5 minutes. Set aside.

In the same saucepan over medium heat, melt the remaining 4 tablespoons of butter.

Add the flour, salt, and pepper and stir until it begins to bubble and thicken, about 5 minutes.

Gradually add the milk and stir until smooth.

Add the garlic, onion, paprika, and nutmeg, and stir for 30 seconds.

Add the mushrooms and stir for 30 more seconds, or until the mushrooms are hot.

Remove from the heat and add a dash of white wine, if using.

Serve over brown rice or noodles.

Pepper

Native to South India's Malabar Coast, pepper dates back to 3,000 years ago, when it was the most valuable spice in the spice trade. Once called black gold, it was even used as a form of currency: Imagine using pepper to pay your rent! The pepper, picked from the flowering vine of the *Piperaceae* family, is actually a fruit, known as a peppercorn. It is picked while still green and then dried. When ripe, the fruit is dark red. Black pepper is the cooked and dried unripe fruit. Green pepper is the *un*cooked dried unripe fruit, and white pepper is the seed from the ripe fruit. The spicy "pep" in pepper comes from the chemical piperine, which is different from the chemical capsaicin, found in the chile pepper. Piperine contains only 1 percent of the spice of capsaicin. Pink peppercorns come from an entirely different plant, the Peruvian peppertree, which is related to the cashew tree and can actually cause allergic reactions in those allergic to nuts.

In the Kitchen *Since freshly ground pepper tastes so much better than preground, and peppercorns and grinders are so widely available today, there's no excuse not to use it. Black pepper, like salt, can bring out the flavors of a dish without changing its character. Add freshly ground black pepper to salads, cauliflower, potatoes, or other buttered vegetables, or grind it over shellfish, salmon, or any other fish. Press fresh peppercorns into steaks. White pepper tastes slightly hotter and sweeter since it's missing the fruit's outer layer, which gives black pepper its more woodsy, pine quality. Use white pepper in cream sauces and mashed potatoes when you don't want black flecks.*

REGIONAL STAR

Used everywhere. Try caramelizing black pepper with soy sauce for a Chinese fried tofu dish. Or try mixing white and black pepper together, as the French do in their mignonette pepper. Black pepper is essential in spice mixes like Ethiopian berbere, Indian garam masala, North African *ras el hanout*, and French *quatre épices*.

HEALING POWER

Pepper is warming and an appetite stimulant. Black pepper folk remedies from the fifth century claimed that pepper cured illnesses such constipation, earache, gangrene, heart disease, hernia, hoarseness, indigestion, insect bites, insomnia, joint pain, liver problems, lung disease, oral abscesses, sunburn, tooth decay, and toothaches. No current medical research supports this, though it is used in Indian Ayurvedic medicine in massage oils for inflammation and as a cure for coughs, colds, and sore throats.

WHERE TO BUY IT: Common black pepper: available everywhere. Pink and green peppercorns: specialty grocery store. White pepper: supermarket, specialty grocery store, online.

HOW TO STORE IT: Buy fresh peppercorns and grind as needed. Whole peppercorns last a year.

COMPLEMENTS

cheese
cherries
cream sauces
eggs
gravies
lemon
pickles
potatoes
salad dressings
salads
stocks
strawberries
tomatoes
vinegar

PAIRS WELL WITH

basil
cardamom
cinnamon
cloves
coriander
garlic
nutmeg
parsley
rosemary
salt
thyme

FLAVOR PROFILE: *warm and spicy with notes of woodsy clove*

Black Pepper Tofu

Prep time: 15 minutes | Cook time: 30 minutes

Serves 2 *People have tried all sorts of ways to try to make tofu taste good. One physicist even tried wrapping it in bacon and freezing it so that as it expanded, the tofu would soak up the bacon flavor. This popular new dish finally succeeds in making tofu taste really delicious.*

1 pound extra-firm tofu
Vegetable oil, for frying
2 tablespoons cornstarch
4 tablespoons butter
4 shallots, chopped
6 garlic cloves, minced
2 tablespoons minced ginger
½ teaspoon ground cayenne pepper
3 tablespoons soy sauce
1 tablespoon sugar
2 tablespoons freshly ground black pepper
6 green onions, finely chopped

Drain the tofu, wrap it in a clean cloth, and press it between 2 cutting boards to squeeze out any excess water.

In a large frying pan over medium-high heat, pour the oil to a depth of about half an inch.

On a large plate, cut the tofu into 1-inch cubes and coat them in the cornstarch.

When the oil is hot, working in batches, use tongs to fry the tofu cubes until golden brown on the bottom, about 6 minutes. Flip and fry until golden brown on the other side, about 4 minutes.

Transfer the cooked tofu cubes to a paper towel-lined plate, and fry the remaining tofu.

Discard the oil into another container to cool down before throwing it out.

Put the skillet back on the burner and melt the butter.

Add the shallots, garlic, ginger, and cayenne pepper.

Stirring occasionally, cook for 12 to 15 minutes, until soft.

Add the soy sauce, sugar, black pepper, green onions, and tofu.

Stir and cook for about a minute with the green onions.

Serve hot over rice.

Black Pepper, Mustard, and Garlic Salad Dressing

Prep time: 5 to 10 minutes

Serves 4 to 6 *This garlicky pepper salad dressing is delicious and full of antioxidants. Toss it over any fresh green salad. It especially brings out the flavors of arugula, beets, tomatoes, and avocados. If the garlic is too intense, use one clove instead of two.*

2 small garlic cloves, crushed
1 tablespoon Dijon mustard
½ cup extra-virgin olive oil
¼ cup balsamic vinegar
¼ cup freshly squeezed lemon juice
1 tablespoon mayonnaise
½ teaspoon sugar
1 teaspoon freshly ground black pepper
1 teaspoon tahini (optional)

In a large jar, shake together the garlic, mustard, olive oil, vinegar, lemon juice, mayonnaise, sugar, pepper, and tahini (if using) until the mixture emulsifies.

Let sit for 10 minutes before drizzling over salad.

TIP: Some people prefer a sweeter version and add a little more sugar and less lemon to bring out the flavor of the balsamic vinegar. Play with the seasoning ratios to find your perfect mix.

Poppy

The urban myth that eating a poppy seed muffin may result in a positive drug test is true. Quite a few people have actually lost their jobs because they ate too many poppy seed bagels before a drug test. These crunchy, nutty seeds contain elements of codeine and morphine, and though the poppy seed consumer won't feel the effects of these opiates, they can be detected in urine. For this reason, prisons in the United States have outlawed poppy seeds, and those on parole must sign a form agreeing not to eat them. In poppy seed folklore, poppies have been used to promote fertility, increase wealth, induce sleep, and even make you invisible, though the latter may have been dreamed up after ingesting the opiate version, which is harvested from unripe poppy seed pods. Poppy seeds are high in essential fatty acids, and one teaspoon of the seeds contains only about 50 calories, slightly less than chocolate.

In the Kitchen *Poppy seeds are most commonly used in breads, pastries, and cakes. Ground poppyseed paste mixed with butter, milk, sugar, and any combination of lemon, orange, rum, vanilla, cinnamon, almonds, walnuts, and chocolate makes a wonderful filling for pastries. Poppy seed paste is best ground fresh (store-bought varieties are usually unusable), but the seeds are difficult to grind, so soaking them in hot water for two hours first and then grinding them in a coffee grinder is recommended. For a savory dish, combine the seeds with lemon, garlic, butter, and walnuts, and add to pasta. They are tasteless when raw, so try toasting them and then sprinkling them over salads or a carrot soup.*

❋ REGIONAL STAR

In Indian cuisine, an ivory-colored variety of poppy seeds is added to kormas, masalas, and coconut milk dishes for thickness, texture, and flavor. The European variety of poppy seed is dark gray in color, and the Turkish variety is brown. Poppy seed pastries are especially popular in Eastern Europe, Israel, Austria, and Germany.

✚ HEALING POWER

High in calcium, iron, magnesium, and omega-3 fatty acids, poppy seeds are cooling and known to reduce fever and inflammation as well as help with sleep. Grind the seeds and add them to a little milk and honey for a calming facial mask.

WHERE TO BUY IT: supermarket, specialty grocery store, online

HOW TO STORE IT: up to six months in a cool, dry, dark place in an airtight container (because of their high oil content, they can easily go rancid) or in the freezer

COMPLEMENTS

almonds

breads
Brussels sprouts
carrot soups
cauliflower
chicken
chocolate
lemon cake
oranges
potatoes
rum
salad dressings
walnuts

PAIRS WELL WITH

cinnamon
masala spices
vanilla

FLAVOR PROFILE: *crunchy and nutty with almond-like notes*

Eastern European Poppy Seed Cake

Prep time: 15 minutes, plus 1 hour to soak the poppy seeds | Cook time: 1 hour, 15 minutes

Serves 8 *Serve this poppy seed cake with tea, chai, or Cardamom Coffee (here). Soaking the poppy seeds and then pulsing them in a food processor releases their flavor. If you like, you can also toast them first. Try replacing the lemon zest with almond extract.*

1 cup boiling water
1 cup poppy seeds
1 cup butter, at room temperature
1½ cups sugar
4 eggs
1 cup sour cream
1 teaspoon vanilla
1 teaspoon lemon zest
2 cups all-purpose flour
1 teaspoon baking soda
1 teaspoon baking powder
½ teaspoon salt
Powdered sugar, for dusting

In a large bowl, pour the boiling water over the poppy seeds. Let them sit for an hour.

When the poppy seed mixture is cool, in a food processor, pulse the poppy seeds a few times, until they are slightly crushed.

Preheat the oven to 350°F.

Lightly grease and flour a 9-inch tube pan (also known as an angel food cake pan). You can also use a square baking pan.

In the large bowl, blend the butter and sugar together and add the poppy seed mixture.

Add the eggs one at a time, beating well after adding each one.

Mix in the sour cream, vanilla, and lemon zest.

In a small bowl, mix together the flour, baking soda, baking powder, and salt.

Bake for 1 hour and 15 minutes (less if using a square baking pan). Check for doneness after an hour by inserting a toothpick into it. The toothpick should come out clean.

When done, cool for 5 minutes and then remove the cake from the pan. (If you are using a square baking pan and the cake is difficult to remove, just leave it in the pan.)

Dust with powdered sugar and serve.

Rich Curry Chicken with Poppy Seeds

Prep time: 15 minutes | Cook time: 30 minutes

Serves 4 *Two sets of whole and dry roasted masalas (spices), including almost every spice in this book, are ground and combined to create this particularly spice-rich gravy. If you can't find the white variety of poppy seed, use the more commonly available black.*

4 tablespoons poppy seeds
½ teaspoon oregano seeds
1 teaspoon mustard seeds
1 teaspoon ground fenugreek
3 tablespoons extra-virgin olive oil
2 cinnamon sticks
10 cloves
⅔ cup chopped onions
⅔ cup finely chopped coconut
6 whole red chiles
5 teaspoons coriander seeds
1 teaspoon black peppercorns
6 green cardamom seeds
¼ teaspoon ground nutmeg
¼ teaspoon ground mace
6 tablespoons vegetable oil
½ cup diced tomatoes
1 (2-to-3-pound) chicken, skinned and cut into 8 pieces
¾ cup coconut milk
2 tablespoons freshly squeezed lemon juice
Salt

In a large, dry pan over medium-high heat, roast the poppy seeds, oregano seeds, mustard seeds, and fenugreek until the aroma starts to bloom, about 2 minutes. Remove from the pan and cool.

In the same pan over medium-high heat, heat the olive oil and sauté the cinnamon and cloves for 30 seconds. Add the onions and coconut and sauté until golden brown, about 5 minutes. Add the chiles and coriander seeds and stir until the chiles begin to crackle, about 2 minutes. Remove the mixture and cool.

In a blender, blend the roasted spices, the sautéed spices, and the peppercorns, cardamom seeds, nutmeg, and mace, and add enough water to make a fine paste, about 1½ cups.

In a large saucepan over medium heat, heat the vegetable oil, add the tomatoes and the curry paste, and cook for 2 minutes.

Add the chicken and 1⅔ cups water, bring to a boil, and simmer until tender, 15 to 20 minutes.

Add the coconut milk and lemon juice, and bring to a boil.

Season with salt and serve over rice.

TIP: This recipe illustrates how the Indian tradition of dry roasting spices and blending them with spices sautéed in oil creates a rich flavor combination.

Saffron

Ninety percent of the world's saffron is grown in Iran. It takes 75,000 flowers from the saffron crocus to make one pound of saffron. That pound will cost you from $1,000 to over $5,000, depending on the grade, making it the most expensive spice in the world. In the Middle Ages, adulterating saffron with other substances to increase its weight was punishable by death. One reason for its high price is that the stigmas of the flowers must be individually handpicked during the single week a year when they bloom. Fortunately you don't need very much—only a few strands. With a taste similar to hay, saffron is prized more for its vivid crimson color, which dyes textiles as well as food. One thread can dye 10 gallons of water. Nevertheless, it has a complex flavor that no one has ever managed to replicate. Consider that saffron contains 150 aromatic volatile compounds compared to fennel's 25.

In the Kitchen *Adding a few strands of saffron is a little like adding gold to your food—you can't help feeling luxurious. Add saffron early to dishes to infuse color; add it later to infuse aroma. Indian safflower sometimes masquerades as saffron, so you're better off buying it from a trusted source. If you can't find Iranian saffron, the next best grade is Spanish saffron. If saffron is going to be the main character in your dish, you're better off getting the highest grade possible, but if it's mixed with other spices, the lower grades will do. Saffron can be added to savory dishes as well as to the same types of cakes, puddings, and custards that include vanilla.*

REGIONAL STAR

Saffron can be found in the paellas of Spain, risotto of Italy, French bouillabaisse, and in a North African pilaf with carrots, onions, and raisins. India also makes a saffron ice cream, and in Sweden, the festival of lights is celebrated with saffron buns.

HEALING POWER

A traditional medicinal antibacterial, saffron can treat coughs and bronchitis and enhance moods, though it is probably too expensive to be a viable medicine.

WHERE TO BUY IT: supermarket, specialty grocery store, online

HOW TO STORE IT: In an airtight container, saffron keeps for many years.

COMPLEMENTS

almonds
carrots
cauliflower
chicken
cream

custards
mayonnaise
mushrooms
onions
Parmesan cheese with pasta
pilaf
pistachios
potatoes
puddings
seafood
spinach
wild game
winter squash

PAIRS WELL WITH

anise
cinnamon
cumin
rose water
shallots

FLAVOR PROFILE: *earthy with hints of grass or musky hay and notes of sharp honey*

Prep time: 20 minutes | Cook time: 35 minutes

Serves 8 *This paella is made with chicken breasts, chorizo sausage, and shrimp. It's an easier variation than the traditional Spanish paella, which includes variations of lobster, clams, mussels, pork fat, squid, cod, and rabbit—but feel free to add any of those ingredients if you have them.*

6 tablespoons extra-virgin olive oil, divided
1½ teaspoons ground paprika, divided
Salt
Freshly ground black pepper
2 pounds chicken breasts, skinned, deboned, and cut into pieces
3 garlic cloves, crushed
1 teaspoon ground cayenne pepper
2 cups uncooked Arborio rice or short-grain white rice
Pinch saffron threads, pulverized in a coffee grinder or using a mortar and pestle or the back of a spoon
1 bunch flat-leaf parsley, chopped
1 bay leaf
3 cups chicken (or fish) stock
1 cup white wine
2 lemons, zested and cut lengthwise into wedges
1 onion, chopped
1 red bell pepper, seeded and cut into strips
¾ pound chorizo sausage, cut into ¼-inch rounds
1 pound shrimp, peeled and deveined
½ cup fresh or thoroughly defrosted frozen peas

In a medium bowl, mix together 2 tablespoons of olive oil and 1 teaspoon of paprika, and season with salt and pepper. Stir in the chicken pieces, cover, and refrigerate.

In a large frying pan over medium heat, heat 2 more tablespoons of olive oil. Stir in the garlic, cayenne, and rice until the rice is coated with oil.

Stir in the saffron threads, the remaining ½ teaspoon of paprika, and the parsley, bay leaf, chicken stock, white wine, and lemon zest.

Bring to a boil. Cover, reduce the heat to medium-low, and simmer for 20 minutes.

In an extra-large pan over medium heat, heat the remaining 2 tablespoons of olive oil.

Stir in the marinated chicken pieces and the onion and cook for 5 minutes.

Add the bell pepper and sausage and cook for an additional 5 minutes.

Stir in the shrimp and cook until both sides are pink, about 3 minutes, depending on size; then add the peas.

Spread the rice mixture onto a warmed serving platter. Top with the meat and seafood mixture, and serve immediately with lemon wedges.

Prep time: 10 minutes, plus a few hours to chill

Serves 4 to 6 *This rich ice cream highlights the complex flavor of saffron. The recipe uses pistachio, but try swapping it out for rose water, orange flower water, or ½ teaspoon freshly ground cardamom for a different take.*

2 cups heavy cream
⅔ cup whole milk
⅓ cup finely chopped pistachios
½ teaspoon saffron
4 large egg yolks
⅔ cup sugar

In a heavy saucepan over medium heat, stir together the cream, milk, and pistachios.

Bring to a boil, then turn off the heat and add the saffron.

In a large bowl, using a handheld mixer, beat together the egg yolks and sugar in the bowl for 5 minutes, until creamy.

Reduce the speed to low; then slowly add the cream mixture to the yolks, beating until incorporated.

Cover and refrigerate until completely chilled, a few hours.

Transfer the mixture to an ice cream maker and freeze according to the manufacturer's directions. Keep in the freezer until ready to serve.

TIP: If you prefer, you can also substitute ground poppy seeds for the pistachios.

Salt

Salt is technically not a spice but a mineral. Humanity's fate has been inextricably linked to salt since we stopped being nomads and getting all our salt from the meat of our herds. The word salad comes from when the Romans salted their leafy vegetables, though it is a misconception that the word salary comes from *salt*. Probably the association of this word with salt is due to the fact that the Romans received a salary for *protecting* the salt roads, rather than actually being paid in salt, though salt has also been used as a form of currency. Korean spas also have salt rooms, believed to detoxify the body. And yet the arguments about how much salt is good for you are still ambivalent. The main point is that by cooking fresh food and salting it yourself, you'll consume less salt than if eating processed foods.

In the Kitchen *You can add salt to nearly everything: apples, bananas, beans, lentils, potatoes, tomatoes, even honey. Use sea salt as your default. It goes especially well on cold dishes. For dishes that can withstand a heavier salt flavor, use kosher salt. Pink Himalayan salt brings out the flavor of any food. If you can find truffle salt, it enhances any egg, popcorn, or risotto dish. Some chefs are even making salt platters for fish to retain their moisture while baking.*

�֍ REGIONAL STAR

In French cooking, *fleur de sel* is the top layer of sea salt traditionally gathered by hand from salt-collecting pans off the coast of Brittany, though now other countries also collect this salt. It's considered an artisanal salt, especially good on foods like tomatoes. Traditional Korean cuisine makes "bamboo salt" by roasting salt in bamboo to absorb its minerals, which are considered especially beneficial in soybean soups. In Russia, at weddings and other important celebrations, guests are presented with a loaf of bread and a bowl of salt to dip it in.

✚ HEALING POWER

Though the World Health Organization recommends that adults should eat less than 5 grams of salt a day (Americans, on average, eat about 10 grams a day), some nutritionists are now stating that too little salt is worse than too much. They claim that salt is necessary to balance hormones and reduce stress. In any case, natural rock salts and sea salts, which contain trace minerals, are healthier than the average table salt, whose minerals have been removed (though iodine, also a necessary nutrient, has been added).

WHERE TO BUY IT: supermarket, specialty grocery store, online

HOW TO STORE IT: Additives are usually added to table salt to keep it from caking. When using natural sea salt, put a few grains of uncooked rice in the salt shaker to absorb extra moisture and help break up the formation of any clumps.

COMPLEMENTS

**everything, especially
beans
cucumbers
eggs
meat
popcorn
potatoes
salads
tomatoes
vegetables**

PAIRS WELL WITH

black pepper and almost any other spice or herb

FLAVOR PROFILE: *salty. Black salt has notes of sulfur. Sea salt has notes of the ocean. Himalayan salt has notes of mountain rock.*

Baby Kale Salad with Salty Vinaigrette

Prep time: 5 minutes | Cook time: 5 minutes

Serves 4 *Mature kale is too tough to be eaten raw, but if you can find baby kale, or grow your own, the addition of almonds, cranberries, Parmesan cheese, and a salty vinaigrette will make you view kale in an entirely new way.*

1 teaspoon salt
1 teaspoon freshly ground black pepper, plus more for serving
1 tablespoon Dijon mustard
½ cup extra-virgin olive oil
6 cups baby kale
¼ cup slivered almonds
¼ cup dried cranberries
Juice of 1 large lemon
3 ounces Parmesan cheese, freshly grated

In a small bowl, beat the salt, pepper, and mustard into the olive oil.

Wash and dry the baby kale and put it in a large salad bowl.

Add the almonds and cranberries and toss with the salty olive oil dressing, lemon juice, and Parmesan cheese.

Serve with freshly ground black pepper.

TIP: When cooking vegetables, try salting each individual set of vegetables before adding it to the dish to bring out the individual flavor of each. As a healthy substitute to salt, try adding brewer's yeast, the vitamin B–rich fungus powder, to popcorn, or try Bragg liquid aminos in place of soy sauce.

Chocolate Chip Cookie Sandwiches with Vanilla Ice Cream, Olive Oil, and Salt

Prep time: 5 minutes | Cook time: Baking time for cookies (per recipe of your choice)

Serves 2 *This decadent dessert is served at San Francisco restaurant Sociale. The addition of olive oil and salt makes this rich dish almost criminal. Buy store-bought chocolate chip cookies to make this really simple and quick, or bake cookies beforehand following your favorite recipe or the recipe on the package of chocolate chips.*

4 large chocolate chip cookies
4 small scoops high-quality vanilla ice cream
2 tablespoons extra-virgin olive oil
Sea salt

Place 1 scoop of ice cream on a cookie and press another cookie on top.

Drizzle the top with olive oil and add a pinch of salt.

Repeat with the third and fourth cookie.

Serve immediately.

TIP: You can also leave out the cookie and just add a little olive oil and salt to a scoop of ice cream or a rich slice of chocolate oblivion cake. For a fruit dessert, try a pinch of salt and some chili pepper on a melon like cantaloupe.

Sesame

Assyrian legend says that when the gods assembled to create the world, they drank wine made from sesame seeds. More likely they added sesame seeds *to* wine to marinate their beef satay, because any search for a sesame wine recipe proves fruitless. The sesame seed is ancient, though, and was the first oil-producing crop. Heat and drought resistant, it grows where no other crops can, like at the edge of a desert. Three thousand years ago, Mesopotamia and the Indian continent were already using it in trade. The magic words "Open sesame" from *The Thousand and One Nights* likely come from the popping sounds the sesame seed makes when it opens. There are two types of sesame seeds: black and tan. In Asia, black sesame seeds are more commonly used, and the Cantonese believe that eating them will prevent your hair from turning gray.

In the Kitchen *McDonald's buys 75 percent of Mexico's sesame seed crop to sprinkle over their buns. Sprinkling breads with sesame dates back to the ancient Egyptians and Babylonians and continues in the Middle East today. They're not just for breads, though. Try them on cabbage coleslaw, steamed carrots, broccoli and asparagus, noodles, rice, salad greens, avocados, bananas, or added to granola with coconut. Sesame seed oil is better as a seasoning than a cooking oil since it burns easily, but because the flavor is strong, it's best to become familiar with its unique toasty flavor before using it.*

�֎ REGIONAL STAR
In the Middle East, ground sesame seed is used to make tahini paste, which is used in salad dressings and sauces for falafel and is one of the essential ingredients of hummus. In Togo, the ground seeds are made into a soup. In Asia, black sesame seeds are not generally ground into paste: Japanese chefs sprinkle them on sushi and salads, Koreans marinate meat with roasted sesame seeds and oil, and Chinese chefs use them in dim sum.

✚ HEALING POWER
High in essential fatty acids, protein, vitamins, and minerals. Sesame seeds are especially high in copper, which can provide relief for arthritis. Ayurvedic massage oils use sesame oil for the nervous system and circulation. Raw sesame oil is useful for those with dry skin conditions.

WHERE TO BUY IT: grocery store, specialty store, online; can be bought in bulk

HOW TO STORE IT: Because of their high oil content, sesame seeds can go rancid. Store in an airtight container or freeze. Raw sesame seeds last about a year, and roasted sesame seeds last about two years.

COMPLEMENTS

bitter greens
chickpeas
coleslaw
eggplant
granola
honey
lemon
miso
noodles
rice
salads
soy sauce
spinach
tofu

PAIRS WELL WITH

cardamom
cilantro
cloves
ginger
pepper

FLAVOR PROFILE: *The seeds are not aromatic when raw but are rich, buttery, nutty, and earthy after being dry roasted.*

Coleslaw with Sesame-Tahini Dressing

Prep time: 15 minutes

Serves 4 to 6 *This coleslaw uses three different forms of sesame: sesame seeds, sesame oil, and sesame paste (tahini). Use a combination of red and green cabbage to create a colorful presentation.*

FOR THE DRESSING
⅓ cup tahini (available at Middle Eastern markets and most health food stores)
1 tablespoon toasted sesame seed oil
Juice of 1 lemon
1 teaspoon minced ginger
Salt
Freshly ground black pepper

FOR THE COLESLAW
6 cups finely shredded or chopped cabbage
2 carrots, grated
2 green onions, thinly sliced
½ cup fresh cilantro
2 tablespoons toasted sesame seeds

In a small bowl, beat together the tahini, sesame seed oil, lemon juice, and ginger, seasoned with salt and pepper, until smooth.

In a large bowl, toss together the cabbage, carrots, green onions, cilantro, and toasted sesame seeds.

Pour the dressing over the salad, mix well, and serve.

Korean-Style Fried Mackerel with Sesame Dipping Sauce

Prep time: 5 minutes | Cook time: 6 minutes

Serves 2 *Korean food is generally known to be spicy and garlicky. Here is a traditional Korean dish that complements the flavor of fish with a simple soy sauce and sesame dressing. Some people don't like a whole fish with the head and tail still attached, but since the fish suggested here are small, you won't find them that intimidating.*

FOR THE DIPPING SAUCE
¼ cup soy sauce
2 green onions, thinly sliced
1 teaspoon rice wine vinegar
⅛ teaspoon sugar
1 tablespoon sesame seeds

FOR THE FISH
Salt
Freshly ground black pepper
2 or 3 whole mackerel, head and tail still attached
Vegetable oil, for frying

TO MAKE THE DIPPING SAUCE
In a medium bowl, mix together the soy sauce, green onions, vinegar, sugar, and sesame seeds.

Divide into 2 small serving bowls.

TO MAKE THE FISH
Salt and pepper the fish, leaving on the head and tail.

In a large pan over medium-high heat, heat the oil.

Add the fish and fry for about 3 minutes on each side.

Serve with the dipping sauce.

TIP: Korean cooking uses two different types of condiments. One is considered a flavoring or spice; the other is considered a decoration. Flavorings include salt, soy sauce, soy paste, pepper paste, sugar, honey, ginger, mustard, wine, vinegar, sesame oil, sesame seeds, garlic, green onion, and shrimp sauce. Their goal is to marinate the dishes so that the original flavor of the food emerges from the inside. Decorative condiments include eggs, parsley, pepper, pine nuts, mushrooms, ginkgo seeds, and walnuts.

Star Anise

Anise Seed

Though these spices are native to different regions, they are profiled together because their taste is so similar and you can substitute one for another. Like fennel, both anise and star anise contain anethole, which gives them their characteristic licorice aroma and flavor. Since star anise is stronger, a good ratio for substitution is one teaspoon of anise seed for every two star anise seeds. Star anise seeds come from the beautiful star-shaped fruit of an evergreen tree native to Vietnam and Southern China. Star anise is used in the cuisines of those regions, but its primary use is in the manufacturing of the antiflu medicine Tamiflu. Anise seed, related to caraway and fennel, is native to the Mediterranean and West Asia and is used in making candies and drinks. The ancient Romans made a cake with it as a post-meal digestive, a possible precursor to the tradition of serving cake after meals today—though our cakes are typically less suitable for digestive aid.

In the Kitchen *Add these spices at the beginning of the cooking process. Add the whole star anise to a chicken broth at the start of cooking, or coat a chicken with anise seed and some salt and bake it. It's also good on root vegetables, with cabbage, in cranberry sauce, or in a cake with figs and almonds, bread puddings, or baked apples. Try it in a fish stew, rhubarb pie, or a marinade with orange juice and pine nuts.*

REGIONAL STAR

In Indian cuisine, anise seeds and fennel seeds are considered the same thing and are often included in fish curries and lentil dishes. Chinese chefs braise pork and poultry in star anise with soy sauce, and it's one of the base spices in the Chinese five-spice blend. Vietnam uses it in their pho dishes. In the West, it flavors some cakes and drinks like ouzo, raki, absinthe, sambuca, and Jägermeister. It's also used to flavor Thai iced tea.

HEALING POWER

antioxidant and antifungal properties. It has also been used to help with colic but is not recommended to take in tea form because the Japanese version of star anise (often indistinguishable from the Chinese form) has been known to cause seizures.

WHERE TO BUY IT: supermarket, specialty grocery store, online. Star anise is usually cheaper than anise seeds, though it's harder to find in the West.

HOW TO STORE IT: Buy star anise whole, and grind it to preserve the flavor. It will keep whole in an airtight container for two years.

COMPLEMENTS

applesauce
beets
bitter greens
cauliflower
dates
figs
maple syrup
marinades
noodles
orange
pineapple
plums
pumpkins
raisins
rhubarb
soy sauce

PAIRS WELL WITH

allspice
bay leaf
black pepper
Chinese five-spice powder
cinnamon
curry leaves
ginger
mint

FLAVOR PROFILE: *both star anise and anise seed have a spicy licorice flavor, though star anise is stronger.*

Simple Anise Seed Chicken

Prep time: 5 minutes | Cook time: 2 to 3 hours

Serves 4 *This roasted chicken, inspired by Mennonite cooking, is coated with anise seeds, which make the skin stick to the chicken and impart a magnificent licorice flavor. Blending with the chicken's natural juices, the seeds help create a rich, deep gravy.*

1 whole chicken
Salt
Freshly ground black pepper
Anise seeds or ground star anise (enough to coat the whole chicken)

Preheat the oven to 300°F.

Salt and pepper the chicken lightly, and coat it with the anise seeds.

Roast for 2 to 3 hours, until done and tender.

Serve with roasted vegetables and the drippings from the chicken.

Prep time: 20 minutes | Cook time: 30 to 40 minutes

Serves 4 to 6 *This recipe is perfect for an autumn or winter side dish. For more color, you might add purple and red potatoes. Consider including other root vegetables, too, like rutabagas or parsnips.*

Extra-virgin olive oil, for greasing and drizzling
8 to 10 beets, cut into ½-inch chunks
3 carrots, cut into 1-inch slices
1 onion, cut into chunks
4 garlic cloves, coarsely chopped
Salt
Freshly ground black pepper
1 teaspoon anise seed or one ground star anise
Juice of 1 lemon

Preheat the oven to 400°F.

Grease the baking tray with olive oil and spread the beets, carrot, onions, and garlic in one layer.

Drizzle the olive oil over the vegetables until it covers them, season with salt and pepper, and sprinkle on the anise seed.

Bake for 30 to 40 minutes, until the beets are tender and can be pierced easily with a fork.

Squeeze the lemon juice over the beets and serve.

TIP: For a dipping sauce, mix 2 tablespoons mayonnaise into ½ cup yogurt. Add ½ teaspoon anise seed and season with salt and freshly ground black pepper. For a more savory dish, substitute sprigs of thyme for the anise seed.

Sumac

The word *sumac* can be traced back to its medieval French, Latin, and Syrian origin meaning *red*. The distinctly bright red colors of the berries make them suitable for ornamental purposes more than culinary, and they're also used for dyeing. Sumac tannins are used to dye Moroccan leather. Sumac is from the *Rhus* genus and distantly related to poison oak, poison ivy, and poison sumac, though it's so distantly related that there is no health risk in consuming the spice. Sumac was widely used in the Middle East before the Romans introduced lemons, and it's still used as a souring agent in many Middle Eastern dishes today. To these cuisines, sumac is the equivalent of lemon to Western cuisine and tamarind to Indian cuisine. In North America, among Native Americans, it is sometimes turned into a sour drink called "sumac-ade." Sumac is exceedingly high in antioxidants, the compounds that protect our cells from aging.

In the Kitchen *Less sour than lemon, sumac's earthy, tart flavor can neutralize the bitter flavor of raw onions in a salad. You can keep it on the table next to the salt and pepper since it's best sprinkled over food before serving. A little like salt, it brings out the flavor of the food, plus it adds a beautiful color and a fresh tartness. It can also be used in dry rubs, marinades, and dressings. Sprinkle it on hummus, or substitute it for lemon when you are looking for an earthier, tart flavor. It is also a good paprika substitute. Sprinkle it on fried potatoes for an alternative flavor to ketchup.*

❋ REGIONAL STAR

Sumac is one of the ingredients in the Middle Eastern spice blend za'atar. It's used widely in Mediterranean and Middle Eastern cooking, especially in Lebanese cuisine on fish. Georgians use it on kebabs and Turks on vegetables. In Turkey it's usually one of the condiments on the table.

✚ HEALING POWER

Sumac is used in traditional folk remedies for ailments including asthma, diarrhea, and bed-wetting. These uses, however, lack scientific backing. It is being hailed as a possible new superfood for its high antioxidant compounds and its possible ability to lower cholesterol.

WHERE TO BUY IT: Some supermarkets, Middle Eastern markets, online

HOW TO STORE IT: Ground sumac lasts a few months. Whole berries can be kept for a year, but they are usually harder to find.

COMPLEMENTS

---

chicken
chickpeas

eggplant
fish
lamb
onions
rice pilaf
walnuts
yogurt

PAIRS WELL WITH

chili
coriander
cumin
garlic
mint
parsley
pomegranate

FLAVOR PROFILE: *sour, fruity, earthy*

Sumac-Tahini Dressing on Avocado

Prep time: 5 minutes

Serves 2 *This avocado snack is a quick energizer. The tartness of the lemon and sumac complement the sweetness of the honey and cut through the richness of the sesame and avocado.*

1 heaping tablespoon tahini
Juice of 1 lemon
½ teaspoon honey
½ teaspoon plus a dash ground sumac, divided
1 tablespoon boiling water
⅛ cup extra-virgin olive oil
Salt
1 avocado, halved

In a small bowl, whisk together the tahini, lemon juice, honey, and sumac.

Add the boiling water and olive oil while whisking until a thin emulsion forms.

Season with salt.

Drizzle the dressing over the avocado halves.

Sprinkle with an additional dash of sumac, and serve.

Prep time: 5 minutes with prepared ingredients

Serves 2 *This hearty salad uses both quinoa and tabbouleh. It's a great way to use leftover tabbouleh. If you don't have any and just want to keep it simple, you can purchase tabbouleh and premade quinoa at the supermarket, as well as the beet sauerkraut. (Wildbrine makes an excellent one.) The blend of the salty, bitter, and sour flavors of the sauerkraut, walnuts, feta cheese, parsley, and sumac are particularly satisfying to the palate. For an extra flavor boost, try roasting the coriander and/or oregano seeds.*

½ cup quinoa
1 cup Tabbouleh (<u>here</u>)
1 jar beet sauerkraut
2 ounces crumbled feta cheese
¼ cup chopped walnuts
2 tablespoons chopped fresh parsley
¼ teaspoon oregano seeds (optional)
¼ teaspoon coriander seeds (optional)
½ teaspoon ground sumac

Prepare the quinoa (see tip).

In a medium bowl, layer the tabbouleh on the bottom, followed by the quinoa.

Layer on the beet sauerkraut, feta cheese, walnuts, and then parsley.

Add the oregano seeds (if using) and coriander seeds (if using).

Sprinkle the sumac on top, and serve.

TIP: To eliminate the bitter flavor, wash quinoa before using. For this recipe, in a saucepan over high heat, add ½ cup quinoa to 1 cup water. Bring to a boil; then reduce the heat. Let it simmer until all the water evaporates. Do not cover. Quinoa, an Andean grain related to amaranth and high in protein, is available at most supermarkets and health food stores.

Turmeric

An ancient Indian medicinal spice, turmeric is now lauded as a superspice for its anti-inflammatory properties. Cancer, heart disease, and Alzheimer's are all caused, in part, by low levels of chronic inflammation, commonly brought on by stress hormones. Curcumin, the active chemical in turmeric that produces its bitter-spicy flavor, also fights inflammation at the molecular level. You have to consume a lot for it to work, usually in capsule form along with a bit of black pepper (which contains the absorption-enhancer piperine), but regularly adding turmeric to your diet can help prevent disease, ease joint pain and arthritis, and help fight depression and aging. Fresh turmeric is sometimes used in cooking, though the dry form is more common. Though related to ginger and also a root, turmeric is brighter in color. Due to its deep orange color, turmeric in Medieval Europe was considered a poor man's saffron. Today it's added as a coloring agent in American mustard.

In the Kitchen *Turmeric is a rather heavy spice to handle alone, but blended with others in a curry powder, it binds them all together beautifully—and just a little gives curry powder its signature color. Add it to rice before it boils for a golden-colored dish. Add it to eggs, a yogurt dip, or a cream sauce to pour over broccoli or cauliflower. Make a dressing combining it with olive oil, lemon juice, salt, and black pepper, and add it to a three-bean salad. Add it to lentil veggie burgers, or use it in a sauce for salmon. Just be careful when using turmeric, because it will stain clothes.*

✳ REGIONAL STAR

In Indian cooking, turmeric harmonizes the flavors in a curry blend, while in North Africa you can find it in tagines and stews. In Southeast Asia, the fresh root is combined with lemongrass, tamarind, chiles, shallots, and garlic into a paste for stews and vegetables; the leaves can be used to wrap up balls of rice.

✚ HEALING POWER

anti-inflammatory and may help fight Alzheimer's disease. Some use it as a face mask, though it dyes your skin a little yellow.

WHERE TO BUY IT: supermarket, online. Fresh turmeric is available in Asian markets.

HOW TO STORE IT: fresh turmeric: in the refrigerator or a cool, dry place up to three weeks; dried turmeric: keeps up to two years in the pantry.

COMPLEMENTS

bitter greens
carrots
cauliflower
chickpeas

lemon
lentils
onions
peanuts
raisins
shallots
sweet potatoes
tofu
yogurt

PAIRS WELL WITH

black pepper
cilantro
cinnamon
coriander
cumin
garlic
ginger
mustard seeds

FLAVOR PROFILE: *bitter, spicy with notes of ginger and woody aroma*

Bill Offermann's Turmeric Salmon

Prep time: 10 minutes | Cook time: 15 minutes

Serves 4 *Salmon aficionado Bill Offermann has tried all types of sauces in which to broil salmon. This one, using a Japanese-influenced method of cooking the fish, is his favorite. Turmeric is often added to American mustard, so why not add it to mayonnaise? The mayonnaise (he recommends Best Foods or Hellmann's) keeps the salmon moist while broiling.*

1 lemon, halved, divided
½ cup mayonnaise
1 teaspoon dried dill weed or 2 teaspoons fresh
1 clove garlic, crushed
¾ teaspoon ground turmeric
Salt
Freshly ground black pepper
Dash ground nutmeg
2 pounds salmon fillet, skinned (if the skin is too difficult to remove, just leave it on)

TIP: When cooking salmon, even 30 seconds can make the difference between an undercooked and overcooked dish. You don't want it overcooked, but you also don't want sushi. It's important to broil the salmon before adding the sauce, so that the fish and not just the sauce gets cooked. For a slightly sweeter version, add 1 tablespoon barbecue sauce. For a unique variation, use 1 tablespoon unsweetened cocoa powder instead of the turmeric.

Preheat the oven to broil.

In a small bowl, blend the juice of half a lemon with the mayonnaise, dill, garlic, and turmeric, and season with the salt, pepper, and nutmeg. The sauce should be bright golden in color.

Place the salmon on a large baking sheet and put it on the top shelf of the oven to broil for 2 to 3 minutes, depending on the thickness of the salmon. You want it to be about halfway cooked.

Take the salmon out and slather it with half of the turmeric mayonnaise.

Broil it again for about 5 minutes, or until the sauce starts to bubble.

Take it out of the oven and flip it, using two spatulas.

Put it back in the oven, without adding more sauce yet, for 2 to 3 minutes more.

Take the salmon out and slather it with the rest of the sauce.

Broil it again until the sauce forms bubbles.

Remove the salmon from the oven and test for doneness by cutting into the thickest part of the salmon to make sure it is cooked.

Cut the remaining half of the lemon into wedges, and serve the salmon with the lemon wedges.

Orange-Turmeric Smoothie with Coconut

Prep time: 5 minutes

Serves 1 *The coconut flakes in this appealing smoothie give it a slight crunch. To make this drink extra refreshing on a hot day, freeze the orange sections before blending. If you can find fresh turmeric root, be sure to substitute it for the dried version.*

1 cup chilled coconut water
2 tablespoons unsweetened coconut milk
¼ cup dried coconut flakes
1 cup tangerine or orange sections
1 teaspoon peeled and chopped fresh or ground turmeric
1 teaspoon peeled and chopped fresh ginger
½ teaspoon vanilla
1 teaspoon honey

In a blender, process the coconut water, coconut milk, coconut flakes, tangerine, turmeric, ginger, vanilla, and honey until smooth.

Pour into a glass and enjoy.

TIP: Try adding 1 tablespoon cocoa powder. For a protein boost, add 1 tablespoon toasted ground almonds or poppy seeds.

Vanilla

After saffron, vanilla is the second most expensive spice in the world. It comes from the bean pod of an orchid originally cultivated by the Aztecs. When Spanish conquistadors discovered the joy of drinking hot chocolate with vanilla, they shipped chocolate and vanilla back to Spain. It was not understood why attempts to grow it in places other than Central America and Mexico were unsuccessful until a Belgian botanist realized that only a native bee and native hummingbird could pollinate the plant. It wasn't until 1841, when a method of hand pollination was discovered, that vanilla began to be cultivated in other parts of the world. Now it also grows in Madagascar and Indonesia. Fresh vanilla beans are actually flavorless: The pods are picked when they are still yellow, blanched in boiling water, dried in the sun, and then wrapped in blankets at night. Only after this fermentation process do the beans develop the intensely smoky, spicy, creamy aroma and flavor for which they are known.

In the Kitchen *Vanilla, also called Bourbon vanilla, has the thinnest beans and a fruity, creamy fragrance, while Mexican vanilla is more spicy and woody. Tahitian vanilla has a shorter, wider bean and is characterized as being more floral. Vanilla extract is used in puddings, baked goods, and custards. The whole vanilla bean can be baked in a pie or pudding and washed and reused. Roast a chicken in a sauce of balsamic vinegar, chicken stock, orange juice, and vanilla, or add it to a vinaigrette with caramelized walnuts. Grind a vanilla bean up with sugar, or add it to French toast, a yogurt smoothie, baked apples, pumpkin pie, or rice pudding. It can also be added to seafood and root vegetables.*

❊ REGIONAL STAR

Mexico makes a hot chocolate with vanilla and cinnamon. French vanilla, rather than a type of vanilla, is the method of blending yolks with vanilla and cream to make French vanilla ice cream.

✚ HEALING POWER

Mayans believed vanilla had aphrodisiac qualities, but there is no evidence to support this.

WHERE TO BUY IT: Whole vanilla beans or vanilla extract can be found at the supermarket, but higher-quality vanilla beans are more likely acquired at a specialty grocery store or online.

HOW TO STORE IT: Store the beans in a dark place in an airtight container. They will keep for over two years.

COMPLEMENTS

---

almonds
apples
bananas
berries

bourbon
brandy
cakes
chocolate
coffee
cookies
cream
custards
French toast
honey
poached fruit
pumpkin
rum
smoothies
vodka
yogurt

PAIRS WELL WITH

cardamom
chili
cinnamon
cloves
ginger
nutmeg

FLAVOR PROFILE: *bittersweet, creamy, smoky*

Homemade Vanilla Extract

Prep time: 5 minutes, plus 3 weeks to 6 months wait time

Varies *Make your own vanilla extract, being sure to use a high-quality bean. They should be dark brown or black, supple, slightly moist or oily, and very fragrant. Though expensive, they make a good investment, because they can be used over and over again.*

1 vanilla bean per ounce of alcohol
Vodka, rum, or bourbon

Most containers of store-bought vanilla extract are about 2 ounces, so you can use that as a guide. If you have an old vanilla extract bottle, use that, or use a larger bottle if you'd like to make a bigger batch.

Slice the vanilla bean or beans in half lengthwise, and put them in the bottle.

Pour enough vodka (or your alcohol of choice) over the beans to fill the bottle.

Seal tightly and store in the dark for at least 3 weeks. The longer you wait, the more potent the vanilla will be. The vanilla will continue to flavor the alcohol for up to a year.

TIP: When you use up the vanilla you've made, you can use the bean again. Or you can continue to add alcohol. Make sure the vanilla bean is always submerged. To ensure this, you can also cut it in half widthwise, making shorter beans.

Prep time: 10 minutes | Cook time: 20 minutes | Total time: 1 hour, 30 minutes

Serves 8 to 10 *With berries, vanilla, and cream, this is the perfect summer dessert. This trifle is so delicious, no one will care what it looks like, but to impress your guests even more, serve it in a glass bowl that allows them to see the layers.*

FOR THE CUSTARD
⅓ cup sugar
2 tablespoons cornstarch
3 egg yolks
2 cups milk
2 teaspoons vanilla extract
2 tablespoons butter

FOR THE CAKE
1 pound mixed fresh or frozen berries
1 cup heavy whipping cream
1 teaspoon vanilla extract
3 tablespoons sugar
1 pound cake
Mint leaves for garnish (optional)

TO MAKE THE CUSTARD
In a medium pot over medium-high heat, whisk together the sugar, cornstarch, and egg yolks. Slowly whisk in the milk.

Continue whisking for 10 to 15 minutes while the mixture heats up and begins to bubble to make sure the bottom doesn't burn and no lumps form.

When the mixture has thickened so that ribbons form on the whisk, remove from the heat and stir in the vanilla and butter. Transfer the mixture to a bowl and chill in the refrigerator for at least an hour.

TO MAKE THE CAKE
If using fresh berries, wash and dry them; halve any strawberries. If using frozen berries, defrost them.

In a medium bowl using an electric mixer, whip the cream until soft peaks form. Mix in the vanilla and sugar.

To assemble the trifle, cut the pound cake into long cubes, about 1 inch by 3 inches. Arrange the cubes to fill the bottom of a glass bowl.

Add one-third of the custard to the cake, one-third of the berries over the custard, and one-third of the whipped cream over the berries. Repeat twice.

Top with the remaining berries and garnish with a few mint leaves (if using).

Unlike the majority of spices in this guide, most herbs flourish in North America and pair well with the foods that grow here. Still, until recently, because they are so perishable, access to fresh herbs was limited to what you grew in your garden. Now that they are so readily available in supermarkets, we are relearning how to use herbs like watercress, arugula, and dandelion that once were considered staples. In the following recipes you can see for yourself in your own cooking how well delicately flavored fresh herbs, like parsley and dill, for example, pair with seafood, and how stronger herbs like bay leaf, rosemary, and winter savory hold up in roasted and longer-stewed dishes.

Arugula

Arugula was popular throughout Europe until the eighteenth century, when it went out of style everywhere but Italy. Now this retro herb is having a comeback. Arugula is part of the bitter green family and has a nutty, spicy flavor similar to endive, dandelion greens, mustard greens, and watercress. These greens are usually slightly less bitter over the winter because sugar acts as an antifreeze for the plant. The hotter the climate, the deeper the summer, and the more mature the leaves, the more bitter these long, lobed leaves become. Arugula is purported to increase sensitivity to touch, and allegedly, monasteries were forbidden to grow it due to its reputation as an aphrodisiac. For this reason, it was sometimes mixed with lettuce, believed to be soothing and to neutralize the excitement arugula instilled. You can usually find it still prudishly mixed with other salad greens in the supermarket.

In the Kitchen *Arugula leaves are so flavorful that a salad dressing of salt, black pepper, olive oil, and a little lemon is all they need. Or make a more extravagant salad by adding apples, avocados, figs, beets, and walnuts with a mustard vinaigrette or with radicchio, gorgonzola, almonds, and a honey-fig vinaigrette. Arugula is also wonderful on a pizza with shaved Parmesan cheese, fig, and prosciutto; with caramelized onion; with fontina, mozzarella, goat, and Montrachet cheeses; or with fennel sausage, goat cheese, and tomato, or substitute it for basil in a pesto with goat cheese instead of Parmesan. Make sure to add it in the final few minutes of cooking because the leaves will quickly wilt, dry out, or lose their flavor in the heat. Its flowers are edible, too.*

REGIONAL STAR

Arugula is regaining its popularity in both the United States and Europe. A quick homemade Italian lunch can be made with coarsely chopped arugula added to hot pasta with grated pecorino cheese and some olive oil. Naples also makes a green digestive liquor from arugula called rucolino.

HEALING POWER

Excellent source of vitamins, minerals, antioxidants, and folic acid. Additionally, some of its chemical compounds have been found to counter carcinogens, helping protect against prostate, breast, cervical, colon, and ovarian cancers.

WHERE TO BUY IT: supermarket in its own bin or as part of a mixed greens combination, specialty grocery store

HOW TO STORE IT: in the refrigerator for a few days. The flavor doesn't keep when it is dried.

COMPLEMENTS

almonds
apples
asparagus
avocados
beets
caramelized onion
chickpeas
corn
cucumbers
dates
eggplant
fava beans
figs
goat and sheep cheeses
hazelnuts
honey
lemon
mushrooms
mustard
olive oil
pizza
quinoa
raisins
red onion
shallots
tomatoes

PAIRS WELL WITH

---

basil
garlic
ginger
green onion
mint

salt

FLAVOR PROFILE: *bitter, earthy, nutty, peppery*

Miguel's Cob Oven Pizza with Gluten-Free Zucchini Dough

Prep time: 30 minutes, plus 10 hours to dehydrate zucchini | Cook time: 15 minutes or less

Serves 4 to 6 *Miguel Elliott, aka Sir Cobalot, aims to bring communities together with his cob pizza ovens. Cob, a mixture of clay, straw, and sand, can be sculpted into a combination pizza oven / wrap-around bench in a park. He has populated the country with many of these ovens, where people can gather together for community pizzas. The following recipe is for his gluten-free zucchini pizza dough, a perfect use for overgrown, dried-out zucchini. You will need a dehydrator to make it, however. Alternatively, you can substitute regular pizza dough for the zucchini dough.*

FOR THE DOUGH
2 large zucchini
Water
Dried oregano (optional)
Dried thyme (optional)
Sea salt (optional)
Minced garlic (optional)
Dried rosemary (optional)

FOR THE TOPPINGS
Arugula
Mozzarella cheese
Prosciutto
Shaved Parmesan, for garnish
Olive oil

Cut the zucchini into slices as thin as possible. You can also use the slice blade in a food processor. Put the zucchini in a dehydrator at 120°F for 10 hours. Before taking the zucchini out, check to make sure it is completely dry. Leave it in for a couple more hours if it isn't crunchy like a potato chip.

Preheat the oven to 400°F.

In a food processor, process the chips into a fine powder. Add enough water to make a thick dough-like texture.

Season with the oregano, thyme, salt, minced garlic, and/or dried rosemary (if using).

Spread the dough thin enough that it covers an oiled 9-inch pizza pan, and bake for 7 to 10 minutes.

Brush the dough with olive oil and top with mozzarella.

For best results, bake in a cob pizza oven for a few more minutes, or bake in a regular oven at the highest setting possible for 5 to 7 minutes, until lightly browned.

Add the prosciutto on top, followed by a large handful of arugula. Sprinkle with Parmesan and serve.

Sweet Potato and Beet Hash Browns with Arugula and Bacon

Prep time: 15 minutes | Cook time: 20 minutes

Serves 2 *This hearty breakfast can be made even heartier with the addition of one or two fried or poached eggs on top of the arugula. Also, make sure to use a nonstick pan for this dish, and include enough oil in the mixture so that the vegetables bind together.*

1 sweet potato
1 regular potato
2 beets
2 carrots
½ onion
Salt
Freshly ground black pepper
¼ cup extra-virgin olive oil plus 1 tablespoon, divided
4 strips pork or turkey bacon, cooked (optional)
2 handfuls fresh arugula, thoroughly washed and dried

Over a medium bowl, grate the sweet potato, regular potato, beets, carrots, and onion.

Season with salt and pepper, add ¼ cup of olive oil, and squeeze the mixture through your fingers until the whole mixture is a little oily.

In a medium nonstick frying pan over medium heat, heat the remaining 1 tablespoon of oil.

Add half of the potato mixture, and flatten it down to cover the pan.

Using the spatula, continue to flatten it into the pan so that the mixture bonds together. Cook for about 10 minutes per side, or until each side is golden brown.

Repeat with the rest of the potato mixture.

Divide the hash browns between 2 plates, put two strips of bacon (if using) and a handful of arugula on top of each, and serve.

Basil

The word *basil* derives from the Greek word for *king*, and many chefs consider this beautifully aromatic plant the king of herbs. Cultivated in India for over 3,000 years, basil is highly regarded there for its healing properties (though not much used in cooking) and is an important herb in Ayurvedic medicine. A traditional holiday in India even celebrates the day Lord Krishna married the *tulsi* (holy basil) plant. Basil is also considered holy in the Orthodox Church because it is believed to have grown from the original cross. In Eastern Europe, many Orthodox churches use basil in preparing their holy water. Belonging to the mint family, basil has 160 varieties, some of them containing volatile chemicals producing flavors for which they are named. For example, cinnamon basil contains methyl cinnamate, the same chemical that flavors cinnamon. Other basils taste of licorice, lemon, camphor, and cloves.

In the Kitchen *Basil is best added at the end of cooking since its flavor diminishes quickly. The two most common varieties are sweet basil, with hints of cloves and anise, used in Italian cooking, and Thai basil, a sturdier, more peppery basil, used in Asian cooking. Sweet basil is best for pesto, salad dressings, and in tomato sauces with garlic. When cooking in tomato sauces, the leaves tend to turn black, but the flavor will still be imparted to the sauce. Try adding fresh basil leaves to a panini with grilled eggplant or to a green goddess salad dressing with sour cream, garlic, and anchovies. Or try a few leaves as a garnish to vanilla ice cream. Basil is one of those herbs that should only be used fresh—when dried, it tastes like hay. However, deep-fried Thai basil makes a nice garnish on any South Asian dish.*

�֍ REGIONAL STAR

Used in Thai, Vietnamese, Cambodian, Chinese, and Malaysian cooking, Thai basil complements garlic, ginger, and coconut milk dishes or stir-fries with garlic and chiles.

✚ HEALING POWER

antioxidant, antimicrobial, antiviral; has been known to ease anxiety and constipation

WHERE TO BUY IT: supermarket (avoid bruised or darkened leaves)

HOW TO STORE IT: In the refrigerator, it keeps for a few days. Or grow in a sunny spot in your garden or on your windowsill.

COMPLEMENTS

sweet basil
artichoke hearts
eggplant
lemon

mozzarella cheese
mushrooms
olive oil
pine nuts
tomatoes
white beans

Thai basil
bamboo shoots
cashews
chicken
coconut milk
corn
shallots
soy sauce
tofu

PAIRS WELL WITH

---

sweet basil
garlic
mint
parsley
rosemary
thyme

Thai basil
chiles
cilantro
garlic
ginger
lemongrass

FLAVOR PROFILE: *sweet with minty, clove, and anise notes*

Tomato, Basil, and Mozzarella Salad

Prep time: 15 minutes

Serves 4 *This salad is best in the heart of the summer, when you can find flavorful heirloom tomatoes. Choose different colored tomatoes for an extravagant, multicolored dish.*

4 heirloom tomatoes, firm but ripe
8 ounces mozzarella balls
Salt
Freshly ground black pepper
Extra-virgin olive oil, for drizzling
1 to 2 tablespoons balsamic vinegar
1 bunch basil, finely chopped, plus a few whole leaves for garnish

Cut the tomatoes into roughly ⅓-inch slices and arrange them on a platter.

Cut the mozzarella balls into ¼-inch slices and distribute them among the tomatoes.

Season the tomatoes and cheese with salt and pepper, and drizzle the olive oil and balsamic vinegar over them.

Sprinkle the chopped basil leaves on top and garnish with a few whole leaves.

Drizzle with a little more olive oil.

Serve with fresh bread for sopping up the juices.

Eggplant with Basil over Polenta

Prep time: 10 minutes | Cook time: 30 minutes

Serves 4 to 6 *This is like a polenta version of lasagna. Kate Frazier, who provided this recipe, prepares this for the monthly homeless meal at a local church. This dish is the one most frequently requested.*

2 tablespoons extra-virgin olive oil, plus more for brushing
1 onion, chopped
1 (16-ounce) can stewed tomatoes
2 tomatoes, chopped
5 cloves minced garlic
4 tablespoons chopped fresh parsley
1 bunch basil, divided
3½ cups water
1 cup polenta
2 cups shredded Monterey Jack cheese, divided
2 tablespoons butter
2 eggplants, peeled
Salt
Freshly ground black pepper
1 tablespoon dried oregano
½ cup grated Parmesan cheese

In a medium saucepan, heat the olive oil.

Sauté the onion until softened, and add the stewed tomatoes, chopped tomatoes, and garlic.

Simmer for 10 to 15 minutes. Add the parsley and three-quarters of the bunch of basil leaves.

In a large pot over high heat, boil the water. Slowly whisk in the polenta. Continue stirring while it cooks, about 7 minutes.

Stir in 1 cup of cheese and the butter, and pour the polenta into an 8½-by-11-inch greased casserole dish to let it set.

Preheat the oven to broil.

Cut the eggplants in half lengthwise, and then cut into ½-inch half-circle slices.

Brush the eggplant with olive oil, season with salt and pepper, and sprinkle with the oregano.

Broil on one side for a few minutes, flip and broil a few minutes more, until soft. Set aside.

Cut the polenta into roughly ¾-inch-thick slices, and lay half the slices, flat-side down, on a platter.

Ladle the tomato sauce over the polenta, and then layer on half of the eggplant, add half of the remaining cheese, and repeat the layers.

Top with the Parmesan cheese and the remaining one-quarter bunch of basil leaves, and serve.

Bay Leaf

The puzzling thing about the bay leaf is why it's one of the most expensive herbs in the herb aisle. While the majority of the other herbs cost about $2.50, a little container of bay leaves costs over $6. Of course, it is an essential herb to add to your stock, but being that it grows so profusely in the moderate and hot climates of North America and the leaves are so easy to harvest, it remains an enigma why they are so costly. It's probably due to the belief that only the Old World Bay Laurel, loftily known as the *Laurus nobilis,* can be used in cooking. But if you live on the West Coast, you know that the California Bay, though stronger, tastes just as good. Actually, bay leaf doesn't really taste that good alone, and you should remove it from your sauces and soups before serving, since the leaves can actually damage the digestive tract. To dry your own bay leaves, place them on a paper towel for a few days until they completely dry; then store them in a jar.

In the Kitchen *Bay is one of those leaves best used at the beginning of cooking. Never use more than one bay leaf per two servings since it can overpower a dish. Crushing it before adding it to the pot will release the flavor more readily, but it will also make it more difficult to remove. Add it to stocks, stews, cream sauces, marinades, rice dishes, and even pickles.*

⁙ REGIONAL STAR

North Africa uses bay leaf in lamb dishes. In France, it is one of the essential ingredients in béchamel sauce and bouquet garni, a bundle of hearty herbs tied up at the stems that can withstand slow cooking. The classic bouquet garni always includes thyme, parsley, and a bay leaf but can also include any combination of basil, burnet, peppercorns, savory, rosemary, and tarragon.

✛ HEALING POWER

antiseptic, antioxidant, digestive; contains vitamins such as niacin, pyridoxine, pantothenic acid, and riboflavin

WHERE TO BUY IT: supermarket, your backyard, a neighbor's tree

HOW TO STORE IT: If you or your neighbor happen to have your own tree, dry the leaves yourself: Simply place on a paper towel for a few days, then store in a jar. Dry leaves keep their flavor for up to a year. Discard if they turn brown.

COMPLEMENTS

beans
black-eyed peas
chili
lentils
mushrooms
onions

pilaf
rice
split peas
stocks
tomatoes

PAIRS WELL WITH

---

allspice
garlic
parsley
savory
thyme

FLAVOR PROFILE: *woody with notes of pepper, pine, and camphor*

Prep time: 1 hour | Cook time: 2 days

Serves 10 *This recipe is from Laurissa Kowalchuk, a chef in Vancouver, British Columbia, who was determined to create the kind of ramen she'd had at some of Vancouver's ramen restaurants. Most ramen chefs offer four different types of broth: miso, red chili bean paste, sesame paste, or black garlic oil. She decided to combine them all. Since this ramen takes so long to make, it's an ultimate comfort food challenge you either pour yourself into wholeheartedly or not at all—chances are, you'll be glad you took the plunge. Note: It's worthwhile to make a lot of broth and then freeze it.*

2 smoked pig trotters
2 chicken necks and backs
1 large onion, quartered
1 garlic clove, plus 1 garlic bulb, minced
10 bay leaves
Handful of peppercorns
2-inch ginger knob, plus 4 tablespoons minced ginger
2 carrots, chopped into chunks
2 celery stalks, chopped into chunks
Handful of Italian parsley stems
Sesame oil, for caramelizing
Butter, for caramelizing
10 shiitake mushrooms, sautéed
Salt
1 tablespoon white miso (per serving)
1 tablespoon chili bean paste (per serving)
1 tablespoon sesame paste (tahini) (per serving)

1 tablespoon mirin (per serving)
1 package plain ramen noodles (per serving)

Sautéed strips of pork belly
2 fresh green onions, chopped
1 hard-boiled egg, halved
Fresh radish sprouts
Black and/or white sesame seeds

In a 10-quart pot filled with water over medium-low heat, simmer the pig trotters, chicken, onion, garlic, bay leaves, peppercorns, knob of ginger, carrots, celery, and parsley stems for 6 hours, with the lid on. For a clearer broth, do not stir.

Strain and refrigerate the liquid overnight.

The next day, use a spoon to remove the fat that has risen to the top.

Put the pot of broth back on the stove over medium-high heat.

While the broth is reheating, in a small pan over medium heat, caramelize the minced garlic and ginger in a mixture of sesame oil and butter for half an hour.

When the stock reaches a soft boil, add the garlic-ginger mixture with the shiitake mushrooms.

Let simmer for an hour, and season with salt.

To prepare soup for 2 bowls of ramen, use 4 cups of broth.

In a small bowl, for each serving, mix 1 tablespoon each of the white miso, the red chili bean paste, the sesame paste, and the mirin (all available at Japanese markets). Add a little broth to make a paste, and then add the rest of the broth (4 cups for every 2 servings).

Boil 1 package of fresh ramen noodles for each serving.

For each serving, ladle soup into a large bowl, add the noodles and the desired toppings, and serve.

Borage

Borage is one of those herbs most people aren't that familiar with, unless you are a gardener using it as a companion plant for protecting and nurturing beans, spinach, tomatoes, and strawberries —then you'll have so much, you'll be wondering what to do with it. Like the herbs burnet and comfrey, borage tastes like cucumber and can be substituted for both cucumber and spinach. Its beautiful star-shaped blue flowers taste like honey and can be added to drinks or cakes. Borage is commercially cultivated for its seed oil, which is sometimes taken as a dietary supplement. In the old days, candied borage flowers were believed to be helpful to those who tended to swoon, and the borage leaves were believed to drive away sorrow and to exhilarate and increase joy of the mind, though this may have been the effect of the wine to which they added it.

In the Kitchen *Avoid the bristly stems, and use the leaves of this herb as you would spinach. Use the younger leaves fresh. Mix them,* finely chopped, with ricotta for a ravioli or lasagna filling, or with parsley and tomato for a chickpea salad. The more mature leaves are best steamed, stir-fried, or added to eggs or soups, such as lentil or split pea—for these, add them at the end of cooking. Or add them to grilled cheese sandwiches, tacos, risottos, or a bacon frittata. Borage's beautiful blue flowers make an elegant garnish for salads, desserts, or drinks. Steeped in water with lemon and honey, the leaves will impart a refreshing cucumber flavor to the lemonade.

REGIONAL STAR

In Iran, a medicinal tea is brewed from borage, and in Turkey, they add it to soup. In Germany, a traditional green sauce called *Grüne Sosse* is made from borage leaves, and the Italians use it in a filling for ravioli.

HEALING POWER

Borage is helpful for gastrointestinal and urinary disorders. It also helps with cardiovascular disorders and promotes better circulation to the heart. It is a good herb for hormonal imbalances and PMS.

WHERE TO BUY IT: Borage is difficult to find. Grow your own or find it at nurseries.

HOW TO STORE IT: Use the leaves within a day of being picked.

COMPLEMENTS

cheese
chickpeas
cocktails
onions
pasta
potatoes
salads

stocks
tomatoes
vegetables

PAIRS WELL WITH

---

dill
fennel
garlic
green onion
mint
mustard
onions
parsley
sorrel
thyme
watercress

FLAVOR PROFILE: *sweetish cucumber flavor with notes of celery*

Markus's "Killa" Martini

Prep time: 10 minutes, plus 2 hours to freeze

Makes 2 drinks *Markus Bennett, martini-maker extraordinaire, provides these detailed instructions for one of the most beautiful (and romantic), carefully crafted martinis you'll ever taste. For the full effect, you will need small star ice trays (preferably the flexible latex type for easy cube removal) as well as medium-size heart ice trays. If you don't have these, they are worth finding. However, you can still make this martini without them. You will also need a zesting tool capable of making 2- to 3-inch strands of lemon peel, and a turkey baster.*

Cranberry juice (Simple Cranberry is Markus's brand choice), for filling ice trays
Juice of 2 lemon wedges, plus keep wedges to garnish
Freshly squeezed pink grapefruit juice (or at least not from concentrate)
Ice cold high-quality vodka (Markus recommends New Amsterdam vodka, excellent quality at an affordable price)
Lemon zest strips to garnish
5 borage flowers for each drink

A few hours before you plan to make the martini, freeze 2 martini glasses.

Fill the star ice cube trays with filtered water and the heart-shaped ice trays with cranberry juice, and freeze.

To assemble the martini, squeeze fresh lemon juice from one of the lemon wedges into each frozen martini glass, and swirl the glasses so that the lemon almost freezes to the sides.

Carefully pour grapefruit juice into the bottom third of each glass. Then fill the rest of the glasses with the chilled vodka, leaving enough room for the forthcoming ice cubes.

Add 4 star-shaped ice cubes to each glass.

Using the turkey baster, dribble just a little cranberry juice onto each star ice cube. The juice will cool and sink to the bottom.

Next, slide a cranberry juice heart onto the surface of each drink. Place a lemon wedge on the rim of each glass.

Sprinkle some lemon zest strips on top of each drink, making sure a few hang onto the edge of the glasses, so they don't all sink to the bottom.

Finally, gently place 5 borage flowers lightly over the surface of each drink, and serve.

Green Sauce or "Herbs of Abundance" Sauce

Prep time: 10 minutes

Makes about 2½ cups *This green sauce is a variation of the German version of green sauce, which traditionally consists of hard-boiled eggs, vinegar, sour cream, and seven fresh herbs, including whatever is in season. The best thing about this sauce is that it tastes different every time. If you prefer to use stronger-flavored herbs like cilantro or basil, use less of them unless you want that flavor to dominate the dish.*

1 bunch borage leaves
1 bunch or more of any of the following: cilantro, sorrel, watercress, chervil, parsley, burnet, lovage, lemon balm, dill, arugula, dandelion greens, or spinach
2 tablespoons or more extra-virgin olive oil (if desired)
Juice of 1 lemon or ¼ cup vinegar
Salt
Freshly ground black pepper
2 garlic cloves, crushed (optional)
½ to 1 cup yogurt (optional)
½ cup cream (optional)
3 hard-boiled eggs (optional)
½ cup walnuts (optional)
1 jalapeño (optional)
1 to 2 avocados (optional)

Wash and dry the herb leaves and purée them all together in a food processor.

Add the olive oil (if using) and lemon juice, season with salt and pepper, and mix well until thoroughly combined.

Add the garlic, yogurt, cream, eggs, walnuts, jalapeño, and avocados (if using).

Serve as a soup, cold or hot. It also tastes great on sandwiches, pasta, cheese and crackers, enchiladas, chicken, or even waffles.

TIP: Every culture has some sort of green sauce. *Chile verde* in Mexico is made with herbs and green tomatillos. The Italians make *salsa verde*, which traditionally includes onions, anchovies, and garlic; and the French make *sauce verte*, flavored with mayonnaise, tarragon, parsley, and/or sage.

Chives

Related to garlic, leeks, shallots, and even asparagus, chives are the only species of onion native to both North America and Europe. They grow prodigiously throughout Europe, from Greece to Sweden to Siberia. Chives look like green onions, but the stems are thinner and have a more delicate flavor. They have pink flowers that can be eaten as well. Though the Romans believed chives could help relieve a sunburn or sore throat, they were not alleged to have magical powers like most other herbs. Chives were not used to crown athletes, attract love, or ward off plagues. This is probably due to the fact that medicinally, they have the same power as very weak garlic, though gardeners have used chives to ward off bugs. Europe only developed its partiality for chives in the nineteenth century, when they became especially popular in Sweden, France, and Poland as a crunchy, oniony flavoring for sandwiches, pancakes, soups, and herring.

In the Kitchen *Chives are best eaten raw to add a crunchy, oniony flavor to potatoes (baked potatoes with sour cream or cold potato salad), fresh green salad, soups (try them in cold cucumber soup), omelets, and cheeses. The pink flowers of chives can also be used in cooking or tossed on salads. Chives can flavor olive oils and vinegars as well.*

✳ REGIONAL STAR

In France, chives, along with tarragon, chervil, and parsley, are one of the *fines herbes*, a blend of delicate herbs often added at the end of cooking. Grown in Europe and North America alike, chives are used in the cuisines of both regions in soups and sauces and over grilled fish. Asia grows a more robust, garlicky variety of chives called Chinese or garlic chives. These are added at the last minute of cooking to stir-fries, fried in bunches for tempura, or used as garnishes in noodle soups, pork, and chicken dishes.

✚ HEALING POWER

rich in vitamins A and C and good for circulation

WHERE TO BUY IT: supermarket

HOW TO STORE IT: in the refrigerator or a glass of water

COMPLEMENTS

asparagus
avocados
butter
carrots
chowders
corn
cream cheese
cucumber

dips
eggs
flavored vinegars
leeks
lemon
lime
mushrooms
olive oil
olives
omelets
onions
potatoes
shallots
smoked salmon
sour cream
squash
tomatoes

PAIRS WELL WITH

basil
chervil
dill
garlic
mint
parsley
tarragon

FLAVOR PROFILE: *delicate onion flavor*

Chive-Infused Olive Oil

Prep time: 5 minutes, plus 2 to 3 weeks to sit

Makes 3 cups *We've added chives to this one, but you can also use other herbs to infuse olive oil, like tarragon. Use this oil in a salad dressing, or drizzle it over focaccia, rice, stir-fries, pizza, baked potatoes, a salmon bagel with cream cheese, or a grilled cheese and tomato sandwich.*

> **3 cups extra-virgin olive oil, or however much will fit into your sterilized bottle (You can also use peanut oil or avocado oil)**
> **1 small bunch chives, washed and dried, with any tough or dried parts removed**

Place the chives in a sterilized bottle.

Pour in the olive oil and cover.

Let sit on a windowsill for 2 to 3 weeks.

You can leave in the herbs or filter them out.

Keep in the refrigerator, and don't worry if the oil becomes cloudy. At room temperature, it will clear up after 20 minutes. Use within a month.

TIP: Alternatively, you can warm the oil in a saucepan and simmer with spices and herbs for about 10 to 15 minutes. You will need about 2 tablespoons of herbs or spices per cup of oil. After it has cooled, strain out the herbs. With softer herbs like basil, cilantro, and dill, crush them first. For heartier herbs like rosemary, oregano, or thyme, you can use the whole stem. Or, try infusing your oil with spices like cumin seeds, coriander, fennel seeds, peppercorns, mustard seeds, or whole cloves.

Cold Bulgarian Cucumber Soup

Prep time: 5 minutes | Cook time: 10 minutes | Total time: 1 hour, 15 minutes

Serves 4 to 6 (medium servings) or 12 (small servings) *This is a more garlicky version of the traditional Bulgarian cucumber soup. Because the flavors are so strong (and delicious), it's a great soup to bring to potlucks and serve as an appetizer in tiny paper cups.*

½ cup walnuts
4 medium cucumbers
2 cups plain Greek yogurt
8 to 10 garlic cloves, crushed
1 bunch fresh dill, minced
1 bunch fresh chives, minced
Salt
Freshly ground black pepper

Preheat the oven to 350°F.

Spread the walnuts evenly on a baking sheet and toast for 10 minutes, stirring halfway through and checking periodically, as they burn easily. Let them cool before crushing them in a coffee grinder or food processor.

Peel the cucumbers and chop 2 of them very finely.

Purée the other 2 cucumbers, and add all the cucumbers to a medium-size bowl.

In a small bowl, beat the yogurt until smooth. Pour it over the cucumber mixture.

Add the garlic, walnuts, and most of the dill and chives, and season with salt and pepper.

Refrigerate for 1 hour.

Serve cold, garnished with the remaining chives and dill.

Cilantro

Cilantro, the Spanish word for the coriander plant, is the more widely used name in North America for the fresh leaves of this plant. Originally brought by the British to Massachusetts in 1670, it was one of the first plants cultivated by settlers. The name *coriander* comes from the Greek word *koris*, which means bug, though it's not clear whether this name comes from its ability to fight them off or for its bug-like smell when unripe. While some cilantro devotees love its zingy, lemony-lime smell, others are repelled by it and think it smells like soap, insects, or even blood. It turns out that people are genetically predisposed to like or dislike cilantro's smell. In the kitchen, such people generally don't understand each other. There's even an online support group called "I hate cilantro." If you've used cilantro before in your cooking, you probably know whether or not this group is for you.

In the Kitchen *Cilantro is one of those herbs that should always be used fresh. The root has more flavor than both the seeds and leaves and can be ground to make Thai curries. Sometimes confused with flat-leaf parsley, cilantro can be identified by its smell—its leaves have a more pungent, citrusy aroma. When cooked, the flavor diminishes rapidly, so leaves should only be added at the end. Mix cilantro with lime into butter, and add it to corn or substitute it for basil in pesto. Or add it fresh to guacamole or any salad.*

⁜ REGIONAL STAR

In Mexican cooking, cilantro is commonly added to beans or mixed with chiles, onions, and tomatoes in salsa. Chinese cooks add it to the rice porridge known as congee. In Vietnamese cuisine, it's used as a garnish for soups and rice wraps. Almost every Georgian dish contains walnuts, garlic, and cilantro. Perhaps this mixture is the reason that Georgians have the highest number of octogenarians in the world!

✚ HEALING POWER

Cilantro leaves are healthier than the seeds. Half a cup of cilantro leaves provides one-third of your daily requirement of vitamin K. The leaves, like the seeds, also have antimicrobial properties.

Cilantro might be useful in fighting salmonella. A natural cleansing agent, it has even helped people with lessening the effects of mercury poisoning. The School of Life Science in Tamil Nadu, India is researching its use in diabetes. It may even help with anxiety and improve sleep.

WHERE TO BUY IT: supermarket, Chinese market. Leaves should be fresh and green and free of any brown spots.

HOW TO STORE IT: in the refrigerator or, if the roots are still attached, in a glass of water. Cilantro leaves last from three to seven days.

Freezing is not recommended.

COMPLEMENTS

avocado
beans
chutneys
coconut milk
cucumber
duck
eggplant
eggs
lamb
lime
meats
onions
pork
salads
shrimp
stews
tomatoes
walnuts

PAIRS WELL WITH

chili
basil
garlic
ginger
mint

FLAVOR PROFILE: *gingery, citrus-like aroma, which either enchants people or repels them*

Badrigiani, or Georgian Eggplant

Prep time: 1 hour | Cook time: 30 minutes

Serves 4 Badrigiani *means eggplant in Georgian, though some call it "goddess dung" because of the green color of the cilantro, and because it is so divine. Traditionally made with walnuts, this is the less expensive "student" version, made with mayonnaise. If you want to try it with walnuts, substitute finely chopped ones for the mayonnaise. This version is delicious, though, and very rich. Serve it with fresh bread.*

2 large eggplants
Salt
Vegetable oil, for frying
½ onion
½ medium-size garlic bulb, or about 4 to 6 cloves
2 bunches cilantro, ends of stems removed, divided
⅔ cup mayonnaise
1 tablespoon *Khmeli Suneli* **Spice Blend (<u>here</u>)**
Freshly ground black pepper

Slice the eggplant lengthwise into ⅓-inch slices. Salt and set aside (see tip).

Pour the cooking oil into a large pan so that it comes up the sides about ¼-inch, and heat to medium-high. Fry the eggplant for about 5 minutes on each side, until golden brown. Be careful of splattering oil.

Set the eggplant on a plate of paper towels. You can layer paper towels on top of the eggplant to add more. Repeat until all the slices of eggplant are fried, adding more oil if necessary.

Sauté the onion until it is golden brown, about 5 minutes, adding the garlic about halfway through. Set aside on a plate.

Remove the skins from the eggplant.

In a mortar and pestle or food processor, purée 1½ bunches of cilantro, including the stems, until a green paste forms.

In a medium bowl, mix together the mayonnaise, green paste mixture, sautéed onion and garlic, and the *Khmeli Suneli* spice mixture. Season with salt and pepper and additional spice mixture if desired.

Slather this mixture over the eggplant and top with the remaining ½ bunch of fresh cilantro leaves. Serve as a spread with bread.

TIP: The hardest part of making this dish is preparing the eggplant. To remove any bitter flavor, salt the sliced eggplant and let it sit in a colander in the sink for 20 minutes. The salt will cause the eggplant to sweat out a brown juice. Gently squeeze each piece of eggplant to extract as much brown juice as possible. This process also improves the texture of the dish when it's fried.

Mexican Black Beans with Cumin and Cilantro

Prep time: 10 minutes | Cook time: 1½ hours

Serves 4 to 6 *For a satisfying treat, dig in to a bowl of these rich black beans with sour cream, fresh cilantro, and lime. Delicious on its own, this hearty dish also makes the perfect game-night dip. If you'd like a little more bite, add a dash of hot sauce.*

1 teaspoon salt
6 garlic cloves, minced
3 tablespoons cooking oil
2 cups black beans
1 cup chopped onion
2 tablespoons ground cumin
6 cups water
1 bay leaf
Freshly ground black pepper
Juice of 1 lime
1 bunch fresh cilantro, chopped, divided
Sour cream, for garnish (if desired)

In a small bowl, mix the salt in with the garlic.

In a large pot over medium-high heat, heat the oil. Add the beans and gently fry them with the salted garlic, chopped onion, and cumin for about 3 minutes, until the garlic begins to brown lightly.

Add the water and the bay leaf to the beans, bring to a boil, and simmer, covered, for 1 to 1½ hours, or until the beans are tender, checking occasionally to see if more water is needed.

Season with salt and pepper, and add the lime juice and half of the chopped cilantro.

Serve with a dollop of sour cream and the remaining half of the chopped cilantro on top.

TIP: Soaking black beans often removes their beautiful black color. Frying them before boiling helps reduce the cooking time a little, removes some of the gases, seals in the flavors of the garlic and salt, and preserves the deep black color of the beans.

Dill

In old English, the word *dilla* means *to lull*, and the herb purportedly derived its name from its ability to ease stomach pain and help with insomnia. Charlemagne even included bouquets of it on his table so his guests could consume it if they feasted too much—or perhaps he adorned his table with it because dill was also considered a sign of wealth. In the West, dill is probably most associated with pickles— the dill pickle is at least 400 years old—but dill is one of the most common herbs used in Eastern and Central European and Scandinavian cooking. The seeds, leaves, and flowers can all be used in cooking, but dill leaves have a quieter flavor than the seeds. Though the seeds are stronger, the flavor of the leaves is more delicate, complex, and fragrant. The leaves look like fennel leaves, but their flavor is not as sweet.

In the Kitchen *Use the leaves fresh at the end of the cooking process and the seeds earlier. The flowers can be added to pickles.*

Add dill instead of chives to baked potatoes with lots of butter or sour cream. Add it to a salad with fresh cucumbers and tomatoes, use it to garnish hardboiled eggs, or for decadent hors d'oeuvres, add sprigs to tiny toast rounds, crème fraîche, and caviar. It's delicious in cottage cheese or dill bread or with a squirt of lemon on salmon or other fish.

⁜ REGIONAL STAR

One of the most widely used culinary herbs in its native region of Russia, Ukraine, and Poland, dill is used to flavor fish, pickles, potatoes, breads, borscht, the cold soup *okroshka*, and the Polish cucumber salad *mizeria*. You will find dill in Scandinavian dishes like marinated herring or with seafood in a creamy sauce with mustard. German chefs combine it with horseradish and use it to braise beef.

✛ HEALING POWER

useful for curing indigestion and hiccups

WHERE TO BUY IT: supermarket

HOW TO STORE IT: Buy dill that looks crisp and fresh, and use it within a few days. Dill seed can be kept for up to two years, but ground dill seed will not keep.

COMPLEMENTS

apples
asparagus
beets
cabbage
capers
carrots
cauliflower
eggplant

eggs
garlic
horseradish
lemon
mayonnaise
mushrooms
mustard
onion
pepper
pumpkin
sour cream
tomatoes
yogurt
zucchini

PAIRS WELL WITH

coriander
garlic
ginger
mustard seed
paprika
parsley

FLAVOR PROFILE: *slightly sweet with notes of caraway, lemon, anise, and parsley*

Prep time: 10 minutes

Serves 2 to 4 *This herbed feta is a great spread on bread or crackers. You can also substitute goat cheese for the feta.*

4 ounces feta cheese
1 tablespoon extra-virgin olive oil
1 tablespoon chopped flat-leaf parsley
4 sun-dried tomatoes, finely chopped
1 tablespoon freshly squeezed lime juice
2 tablespoons finely chopped fresh dill
1 teaspoon finely chopped fresh or dried oregano
Freshly ground black pepper

In a medium bowl, stir together the feta, olive oil, parsley, tomatoes, lime juice, dill, oregano, and pepper.

Serve with crackers or bread.

TIP: To herbify cheese, try other variations of herbal combinations such as rosemary, sage, and thyme; fennel and lavender; garlic and chives; basil and herbes de Provence; or just plain dill and salt.

Russian Borscht

Prep time: 15 minutes | Cook time: 1 hour, 10 minutes

Serves 8 to 10 *There are probably as many recipes for borscht as there are families in Russia and Eastern Europe. Some are vegetable heavy, others are made only with beets, and still others use sausage or pork fat. This vegetarian version oozes with flavor, though you can add bacon or sausage toward the beginning of cooking, if desired.*

3 tablespoons butter
2 carrots, peeled and grated
4 large beets, peeled and grated
2 onions
½ head cabbage, chopped
1 jalapeño pepper, seeded and chopped
6 garlic cloves, minced
2 large potatoes, peeled and cut into ½-inch chunks
Salt
Freshly ground black pepper
2 tablespoons balsamic vinegar
1 tablespoon sugar
1 small bunch fresh dill, chopped, divided
Sour cream, for garnish

In a large pot over medium-high heat, melt the butter.

Add the carrots, beets, and onions, and stir until slightly softened and reduced in volume, about 5 minutes.

Add the cabbage, jalapeño pepper, and garlic, and continue to stir.

Add enough water to cover the vegetables.

Add the potatoes and cook for about an hour.

Season with salt and pepper, and add the balsamic vinegar, the sugar, and half of the dill. Adjust the seasonings as desired.

This soup is better if it is allowed to sit a few hours and then reheated.

Serve with a spoonful of sour cream and the remaining half of the chopped dill.

TIP: This soup is even better the next day after the flavors have blended and matured. Instead of the balsamic vinegar, you can also add red wine. For a less spicy version, leave out the jalapeño. Note that the beets will color your clothes and hands a brilliant magenta, but it washes out.

Fennel

Fennel is one of the herbs in the tenth-century Anglo-Saxon Nine Herb Charm, a salve that when ground with other herbs like mugwort and thyme could cure any wound. Fennel is also one of the three herbs used in making absinthe. The weedy leaves resemble dill but are thinner and sweeter with a licorice flavor from the aromatic compound anethole, the same volatile chemical that flavors anise and star anise, though fennel is slightly milder. Fennel can be found growing wild in the open lands and pastures of North America and Northern Europe. It is called *finocchio* in Italian, and because its flavor is so effective in masking others, to dupe someone in Italian is *infinocchiare*. Even Dante allegedly pronounced, "Those I thought to be friends, were fennels instead!" The herb doesn't really deserve such a negative reputation because it's mainly quite sweet.

In the Kitchen *The fennel leaves, bulb, and seeds (which have the strongest flavor) can all be used in cooking, though different species*

245

of fennel are cultivated to enhance each part of the plant. The bulb can be sautéed, included in stews, or eaten raw in a salad. The seeds are larger than anise seeds but can be mistaken for them because of the similar flavor. Sprinkle them on roasting vegetables. When cooking with the leaves, choose only the fresh young ones. Try baking a whole fish on a bed of fennel leaves, or add them to herring with red onion, clam chowder, or sauerkraut.

❋ REGIONAL STAR

Fennel is seen in Indian cuisine—roasted fennel seeds are offered in most Indian restaurants as an after-dinner digestive—as well as the cuisines of Central Asia, the Middle East, and in the Chinese five-spice powder blend. In Syria the leaves are used to make omelets. In Italian cuisine, fennel seeds are the main flavoring agent in sausages, while the leaves are added to pasta and sardines.

✚ HEALING POWER

High in potassium, vitamin C, beta carotene, and a natural source for estrogen. Fennel aids in digestion and metabolism.

WHERE TO BUY IT: supermarket, specialty grocery store

HOW TO STORE IT: Fresh fennel can keep for a few days in the refrigerator.

COMPLEMENTS

avocado
beets
Brussels sprouts
cabbage
carrots
cheese
cucumbers

eggplant
fish
garlic
grapefruit
lemon
mushrooms
olives
pepper
pickles
pine nuts
red onions
risottos
salads
sausage
tomato sauces
vodka

PAIRS WELL WITH

---

black pepper
cinnamon
coriander
garlic
parsley
salt
Sichuan pepper
thyme

FLAVOR PROFILE: *fresh and sweet with notes of licorce*

Prep time: 15 minutes

Serves 4 to 6 *Everything goes with arugula these days. Try it in this modern version of an arugula salad. Complementary add-ins include beets and hazelnuts, grapefruit and hearts of palm, and sliced pears and almonds.*

FOR THE VINAIGRETTE
2 tablespoons freshly squeezed lemon juice
3 tablespoons freshly squeezed orange juice
1 teaspoon orange zest
½ teaspoon sugar
¼ cup extra-virgin olive oil
1 tablespoon Dijon mustard
1 shallot, chopped
Salt
Freshly ground black pepper

FOR THE SALAD
1 large fennel bulb
4 cups arugula
4 ounces goat cheese
½ cup toasted pine nuts

TO MAKE THE VINAIGRETTE
In a medium bowl, beat together the lemon juice, orange juice, orange zest, sugar, olive oil, mustard, and shallot, and season with salt and pepper.

TO MAKE THE SALAD

Cut the fennel bulb in half; then cut into thin slices, and then crossways to make 1-inch lengths.

In a salad bowl, toss the arugula and fennel with the vinaigrette. Top with chunks of goat cheese and the pine nuts, and serve.

TIP: For additional flavor treats, try adding any of the following fruit and nut combinations: orange or mandarin slices and cashews, walnuts and figs, strawberries, dried cranberries, or pomegranates.

Prep time: 15 minutes, plus overnight to chill | Cook time: 6 to 7 minutes

Makes 12 (¼-pound) breakfast patties *You can use a food processor to grind your own sausage meat. And don't worry about casings for these sausages—just make patties out of them instead. Just add eggs and toast for a hearty breakfast.*

3 tablespoons fennel seeds
1 (3-pound) pork shoulder roast, cut into large chunks, most of the fat removed
1 tablespoon salt
1 teaspoon freshly ground black pepper
½ teaspoon red pepper flakes
4 tablespoons minced flat-leaf parsley
¼ cup Asiago cheese
2 garlic cloves, minced
Extra-virgin olive oil, for sautéing

In a dry pan over medium-high heat, toast the fennel seeds until their aroma blooms. Set aside to cool.

In a large bowl, use your hands to mix together the pork roast, salt, pepper, red pepper flakes, parsley, cheese, garlic, and fennel seeds, making sure all the ingredients are well blended.

Cover with plastic and refrigerate overnight

In a food processor, pulse until the mixture is thoroughly ground.

Form the sausage into patties.

In a large pan over medium-high heat, sauté in olive oil for a few minutes on each side, until there is no pink left in the middle.

Serve.

Garlic

In a traditional Korean folktale, a bear sits in a cave eating nothing but garlic and mugwort until he turns into a human. The moral of the story is that garlic makes you a human. Among herbs, garlic has a kind of cult status. People love it or hate it, but they usually have some sort of emotion about it. As the title of Les Blank's garlic documentary states, *Garlic Is as Good as Ten Mothers*. Festivals are devoted to it where chefs try every possible combination, including garlic-flavored ice cream (kind of like eating vanilla ice cream after a garlic-heavy dinner) or garlic chip cookies. Native to Central Asia, it was first used as a medicinal herb. Its healing powers range from preventing hair loss to reducing cholesterol, lowering blood pressure, and keeping away colds, flu, acne, athlete's foot, mosquitoes, vampires, and even the plague. You can even de-ice your sidewalks with garlic, though better to just stay inside and eat it.

In the Kitchen *Americans today consume more than 250 million pounds of garlic a year. Baking it greatly reduces garlic's spicy bite and creates a subtly flavored paste, which even makes a dish like baked chicken with 40 cloves of garlic possible. Whole cloves of garlic sautéed in a stir-fry also impart a more subtle flavor to the oil than when the garlic is chopped. The smaller it's minced, the stronger the flavor. When garlic and onions are cooked together, add the onions first, since garlic can burn easily. Try caramelizing garlic in a frying pan with balsamic vinegar and adding it to a mushroom cheese tart. Add it to mayonnaise to make aioli, to mashed potatoes, or to melted butter on bread.*

REGIONAL STAR

It's everywhere. You can find garlic pickles in Korea and Russia, and it's sautéed with everything in Asia, including poultry, vegetables, and eggplant. It's used prodigiously in Italian sauces and in the eggplant–bell pepper spreads of Southern Europe.

HEALING POWER

Lowers blood pressure and cholesterol. Wards off colds, flu, and cancer. Antiaging, antibacterial, antifungal properties.

WHERE TO BUY IT: supermarket

HOW TO STORE IT: in a cool, dry place

COMPLEMENTS

beans
bitter greens
corn
eggplant
mushrooms
olive oil

olives
pasta
pine nuts
soy sauce
spinach
tahini
vinaigrettes
vinegar

PAIRS WELL WITH

cilantro
curry
oregano
parsley
rosemary
sage
salt
thyme
turmeric

FLAVOR PROFILE: *pungent, hot, and oniony*

Roasted Garlic and Brie

Prep time: 5 minutes | Cook time: 35 minutes

Serves 2 to 4 *This recipe from the 1980s still tastes great. It works as an appetizer, but the mixture of Brie, garlic, and mushrooms is so satisfying, it can make a full meal, too. Baking garlic lessens its potency dramatically; one whole bulb of garlic is equal to about one clove of minced raw garlic. Nevertheless, after eating this dish, make sure you don't have an important meeting to attend the next day.*

> **2 to 4 heads garlic (1 head per person)**
> **1 tablespoon butter**
> **1 cup mushrooms, sliced**
> **1 baguette**
> **1 (8-ounce) wheel of Brie**

Preheat the oven to 400°F.

Remove the outer papery skin from the heads of garlic and cut off the ends. Put the garlic in a baking dish and bake for about 30 minutes, until soft.

About 10 minutes before the garlic is done, in a medium pan over medium heat, melt the butter. Sauté the mushrooms until golden brown, about 10 minutes.

Slice the baguette and briefly toast the bread.

When the mushrooms are golden brown, unwrap the Brie and plop it into the frying pan with the mushrooms until it melts.

Serve the mushroom Brie in the pan at the table, along with the toast and baked garlic.

To eat: Spread the mushroom Brie onto rounds of toast, and then squeeze the garlic, now a paste, on top.

Immune-Boosting Garlic Tonic

Prep time: 5 minutes

Serves 1 *Imbibing garlic may be useful in preparing for cold and flu season, since it contains compounds capable of killing a wide variety of organisms, including viruses and bacteria that cause earaches, colds, and influenza. Raw garlic, however, though potent in its healing powers, can be tough on the digestive system. The ginger in this tonic helps neutralize that. If you have mint growing in your garden, you could add that as well.*

1 fresh garlic clove
½ teaspoon ground cayenne pepper
1 teaspoon honey (optional)
1 teaspoon crushed ginger root
1 cup freshly squeezed orange juice (or at least not from concentrate)
½ teaspoon ground cinnamon (optional)

In a blender, purée the garlic, cayenne, honey (if using), ginger, orange juice, and cinnamon if using.

Drink immediately.

TIP: The easiest way to peel garlic is to crush it with the flat side of the knife blade. To get the smell get off your fingers, simply rub your hand against the back of a grater under water. Then a teaspoon of fresh lemon juice will help get that garlicky taste out of your mouth. Taking garlic pills isn't as effective as eating raw garlic because the fresh clove must be crushed in order to release the enzymes that help fight off viruses and bacteria. So to "activate" garlic's medicinal properties, make sure it's thoroughly crushed.

Green Onion

Though technically an onion more than an herb, we include green onions in this guide because they have such an important and versatile presence in the kitchen. The long, green, tubular stalks of this plant are also called Welsh onions, Japanese leeks, young onion, onion sticks, salad onions, and scallions, depending on the region. Sometimes people become confused about scallions and green onions because they are two different words for the same onion. And while some think spring onions and green onions are the same thing, spring onions are just regular onions that have been picked before their bulb has fully developed, and they have a stronger flavor. Green onions are available in supermarkets year round. They are also easy to grow. Choose those that are bright green without any wilted stems, and wash off any slimy parts before using them in cooking. They add an oniony flavor to dishes without the intensity of regular onion.

In the Kitchen *The white root of the green onion can be used, but chop off the stringy section, and chop the bulb more finely since its flavor is stronger. When cooking with the stalks, the tough ends should be discarded. Sauté slices of green onion and add them to soups, pasta, stir-fries, omelets, or quiches. Caramelize them like onion and add them to barbecue sauce or cornbread. Milder than onion, they can be eaten raw (thinly sliced) in salads or in deviled eggs. Add them to pancakes or focaccia bread or mix them into a yogurt dip or potato salad. They can also be grilled whole.*

REGIONAL STAR
Green onions are usually mixed with garlic and ginger in Asian cooking, most often at the end of the cooking process. They are used extensively in Japanese, Chinese, Korean, and Thai cuisines. In Vietnam, they are added to a rice porridge to treat colds. In India, a chutney is made from green onion and mint.

HEALING POWER
High in vitamins C, K, and A, a potent cocktail of vitamins helpful in bone, eye, and heart health.

WHERE TO BUY IT: supermarket

HOW TO STORE IT: in the refrigerator for up to a week

COMPLEMENTS

asparagus
beans
cheese
coconut milk
corn
cream
eggplant

greens
lemon
lime
mushrooms
mustard
pasta
potatoes
sesame oil
soy sauce
tomatoes
vinegar

PAIRS WELL WITH

basil
bay leaf
cilantro
dill
fennel
garlic
ginger
lemongrass
mint
parsley
rosemary
sage
sesame seeds
thyme

FLAVOR PROFILE: *oniony with notes of spring*

Prep time: 5 minutes | Cook time: about 8 minutes per pancake

Serves 2 to 4 *The simplest way to make these pancakes is to buy the pancake mix called* pa'jan *mix at an Asian market. While you are there you can pick up some Korean rice wine, called* makuli, *or farmer's beer, and spicy cabbage kimchi, which go excellently with these pancakes. The pancakes should be served sizzling hot.*

¾ cup *pa'jan* mix
1 cup water
1 (16-ounce) package frozen seafood mix (any combination of squid, scallops, and shrimp), thawed
2 bunches green onion, green parts only, cut into 2-inch pieces
2 carrots, chopped into thin slices
1 sweet potato, thinly sliced (optional)
Cooking oil, for frying
3 tablespoons soy sauce
½ teaspoon rice wine vinegar

In a large bowl, beat the *pa'jan* mix with the water until smooth and no lumps remain. It should look like thin pancake mix.

Add the seafood, green onion, carrots, and sweet potato (if using) to the pancake mix, and stir thoroughly.

In a medium pan over medium-high heat, heat about 3 tablespoons cooking oil.

Test the heat by flicking a drop of water into the oil. If it sizzles, it's ready.

Ladle about 1 cup of the mix into the pan, spreading it around with the back of the ladle so the mixture reaches the sides of the pan.

Cook for about 5 minutes, or until the edges look golden brown. Peek under the pancake with the spatula to ensure the pan side is golden.

Flip the pancake and cook for an additional few minutes, until golden. You might need to turn down the heat if the pancake is cooking too quickly.

Repeat until all the batter is used, adding more oil as needed.

In a small bowl, mix the soy sauce with the white wine vinegar, and serve with the hot pancakes.

Prep time: 10 minutes | Cook time: 15 minutes

Serves 4 *After sautéing the chicken breasts in this zesty green onion pesto, add a little extra as a garnish on top. This pesto also makes an excellent addition to rice, rice porridge, or soups.*

2 bunches green onions, green parts only, cut into 1-inch slices, divided
1 tablespoon grated ginger
2 garlic cloves, crushed
2 tablespoons sesame oil
2 tablespoons extra-virgin olive oil
1 pound chicken breasts, cut into bite-size pieces
1 red bell pepper, sliced into strips
2 tablespoons oyster soy sauce
1 tablespoon soy sauce
Juice of 1 lemon
Cilantro leaves, for garnish

In a food processor or blender, process half of the green onions with the ginger, garlic, and sesame oil into a paste.

In a large frying pan, heat the olive oil.

Add the chicken and stir-fry until it changes color, 10 minutes or more.

Add the red bell pepper, oyster sauce, remaining half of the green onions, oyster soy sauce, soy sauce, lemon juice, and 2 tablespoons of the green onion pesto.

Stir-fry for another 2 minutes.

Serve hot over rice, topped with a large dollop of green onion pesto and garnished with the cilantro leaves.

Horseradish

Native to Eastern Europe and Russia, horseradish root is grated with lemon or vinegar to accompany the beef, ham, and suckling pig of those regions. Like mustard, horseradish root has little aroma until it's cut or grated, activating the cells of the plant to try to irritate the eyes and mucous membranes of whomever (or whatever) is trying to eat it. When chefs speak of horseradish, they are usually referring to the prepared version already grated and soaking in vinegar. Horseradish in the United States is often combined with mayonnaise or sour cream to make a horseradish cream, since it's often too hot for North American palates. The leaves have a similar flavor to the root but are milder and can spice up salads. Prepared horseradish is often dolloped on raw oysters—which pair well with Bloody Mary cocktails, also containing horseradish.

In the Kitchen *Prepared horseradish is delicious with cheese, sausages, roast beef, pasta, smoked trout, and in potato and hard-*

266

boiled egg salads. *To make your own horseradish sauce, finely mash 1 cup peeled and cubed horseradish in a food processor. Add ½ cup vinegar or lemon juice and a little salt (just keep your nose and eyes at a safe distance!). It will keep in the refrigerator for many months. Add sour cream and a little mustard for a horseradish cream. Or combine grated horseradish with grated apples and lemon on potato latkes. With mustard and honey, it makes a good glaze for ham, or add it to a ham and cheese sandwich. It's also tasty in mashed potatoes, steamed carrots, or hollandaise sauce, or even on pâté.*

⁘ REGIONAL STAR

One of the five bitter herbs of a seder, horseradish is essential to Passover meals and as an accompaniment to gefilte fish. In Poland, a horseradish soup is served on Easter. In Slovenia, a hard-boiled egg salad contains sour cream, apples, and horseradish, and in many Eastern European countries, beet is included as well.

✚ HEALING POWER

Extremely high in vitamin C and antibacterial properties. Helps digest oily meats and fish.

WHERE TO BUY IT: supermarket

HOW TO STORE IT: The fresh root will keep in the refrigerator for up to three weeks.

COMPLEMENTS

apples
arugula
avocado
beef
beets

cabbage
carrots
cocktails
cream
cucumbers
eggs
greens
ketchup
lemon
mayonnaise
mushrooms
oily meats
parsnips
potatoes
soy sauce
tomatoes
vinegar
yogurt

PAIRS WELL WITH

chives
dill
green onions
mustard
parsley
rosemary
sage

FLAVOR PROFILE: *bitter, hot, mustardy*

Brisket

Prep time: 5 minutes | Cook time: 5 to 8 hours

Serves 8 to 10 *Baking what is usually considered an inferior piece of meat for long hours in horseradish and wine is an excellent way to turn something mundane into something rich and celebratory.*

5-pound cut of brisket
Salt
Freshly ground black pepper
2 tablespoons cooking oil
2 white onions, cut in slices
1 (12-ounce) container of horseradish
1 bottle dry red wine, divided

Preheat the oven to 300°F.

Season the meat with salt and pepper.

In a cast iron skillet over medium-high heat, sear the brisket until it's brown, 6 to 7 minutes per side.

Place the brisket in a baking pan.

In the same skillet used to sauté the brisket, sauté the onions until they are soft.

Slather the brisket with the horseradish and put the onions on top.

Pour half of the bottle of wine over the whole thing.

Bake for 5 to 8 hours, adding more wine as needed. (You can also add beef stock if you use up all the wine.)

The longer you cook the brisket, the better and more tender it will become. Serve warm.

Shrimp Cocktail

Prep time: 10 minutes, plus 15 minutes to chill | Cook time: 5 minutes

Serves 4 to 8 *This simple ketchup-based sauce pairs beautifully with shrimp for an appetizer. Try serving this alongside a traditional Bloody Mary, also made with horseradish.*

2 pounds shrimp, peeled and deveined
½ cup ketchup
1 teaspoon Worcestershire sauce
1 tablespoon fresh or prepared store-bought horseradish
Juice and zest of 1 lemon
Salt
Few drops Tabasco sauce (optional)
1 bunch fresh Italian parsley, chopped
1 fresh lemon, cut into wedges

Bring a large pot of water to a boil.

Drop the shrimp into the boiling water.

Reduce the heat to simmer and cook for 3 to 4 minutes.

Drain the water and transfer the shrimp to a large bowl of ice to chill.

In a small bowl, mix together the ketchup, Worcestershire sauce, horseradish, lemon juice, and lemon zest. Refrigerate for at least 15 minutes before serving. Season with salt, and add more horseradish or lemon juice and the Tabasco sauce (if using).

Serve the cocktail sauce garnished with the Italian parsley and fresh lemon wedges alongside the shrimp.

Lavender

Native to Southern France, where fields of it blanket the countryside, lavender's beautiful purple flowers made it equally popular in English Tudor gardens. Lavender is well known for its use as a bath salt, lotion, and massage oil as well as its abundant nectar that produces high-quality honey. Lavender is also used in eye pillows and aromatherapy because its fragrance soothes anxiety and evens out sleep disturbances. French schoolteachers used to crush up lavender leaves to calm rowdy students. The aroma also deters bugs and other pests. Adding too much to a culinary dish, however, can inundate it with a floral aroma that, for some people, may be a little too reminiscent of a spa, so use it sparingly. If you grow your own, you can dry it by hanging it upside down. Bunches of lavender in baskets make great gifts, especially if those baskets include a lavender-flavored cheese.

In the Kitchen *Though powdered lavender was used in medieval times as a condiment, it is now valued more for its scent, which adds a floral, slightly sweet aroma to dishes. Since it is so potent, a few leaves ground in a coffee grinder are enough to flavor all the salt in your salt shaker. A few leaves can be added to sugar, too, for topping desserts, custards, or scones. Grinding it with the sugar will make a more potent sugar for baking. The flowers are sometimes used to decorate cakes since lavender pairs well with chocolate. Try it on honey with blue cheese and figs or in a rub with rosemary on baked chicken or lamb.*

REGIONAL STAR

Native to the South of France, lavender was not used in traditional French cooking until the 1970s, when spice marketeers invented the herbal blend herbes de Provence. In Morocco, it is occasionally used in the spice blend *ras el hanout*.

HEALING POWER
calming

WHERE TO BUY IT: Buy fresh lavender at garden supply stores and dried lavender at supermarkets, specialty grocery stores, or online.

HOW TO STORE IT: Keep fresh lavender in a plastic bag in the refrigerator for up to a week. Dried lavender will keep much longer.

COMPLEMENTS

apricots
arugula
baked goods
berries
butter
cheese

chocolate
corn
custards
figs
honey
ice cream
lemon
oranges
rhubarb
rice
vanilla
vinegar
walnuts
yogurt

PAIRS WELL WITH

---

basil
caraway
cinnamon
mint
oregano
rosemary
saffron
savory
thyme
vanilla

FLAVOR PROFILE: *bitter and sweet with notes of lemon, mint, and earthy forest*

Prep time: 30 minutes, plus 2 hours to sit | Cook time: 30 minutes

Serves 6 to 8 *This lamb rub is made of lavender along with the herbs that grow in its natural vicinity—the South of France. You can add both the leaves and the flowers of the fresh lavender, bearing in mind that the flowers have a stronger flavor than the leaves. Serve with roasted rosemary potatoes.*

1 lemon, halved
1 (5- to 6-pound) leg of lamb, deboned, fat trimmed
6 garlic cloves, cut into 4 pieces each
1 tablespoon salt, plus more for seasoning
2 tablespoons freshly ground pepper, plus more for seasoning
3 tablespoons fresh lavender flowers and leaves, plus lavender sprigs for garnish
3 tablespoons chopped fresh rosemary leaves
2 tablespoons chopped fresh mint
3 tablespoons extra-virgin olive oil

Squeeze the juice of the lemon over the lamb, rub it in with your hands, and add the salt and pepper.

Make 24 small incisions all over the lamb, and insert 1 slice of garlic in each.

Season the lamb with additional salt and pepper.

In a small bowl, stir together the lavender, rosemary, mint, and olive oil.

Rub the mixture over the lamb and let it sit at room temperature for at least 2 hours.

Preheat a grill or broiler.

Place the lamb on the grill or under the broiler, and cook until golden on one side, about 15 minutes.

Turn the lamb and cook until medium rare, about another 15 minutes.

Remove the lamb from the oven and let rest for 10 minutes.

Garnish with lavender sprigs, and serve.

TIP: Test for doneness with a meat thermometer. It should read 135°F to 140°F when inserted into the lamb. Alternatively, cut into the thickest section. It should be slightly pink but not red inside.

Prep time: 5 minutes | Cook time: 5 to 10 minutes

Makes 1 cup *While most versions of herbal butters just have you whip the herbs into the butter, this recipe uses ghee and heats the herbs to distribute the flavor throughout. This lavender butter is particularly delicious spread on dark bread. This recipe makes quite a bit, so you can even bring a little bowl to share with your neighbor.*

⅓ cup fresh lavender, or 4 tablespoons dried
1 cup ghee

If using fresh lavender, wash and thoroughly dry the herbs and chop them finely.

In a medium saucepan over low heat, gently heat the herbs and ghee until the herbs slightly sizzle.

Strain the mixture through a cheesecloth into a large bowl.

Transfer the lavender butter to small butter bowls, and refrigerate.

TIP: You can buy ghee at Indian markets and some health food stores, or make your own by heating up butter until it bubbles and the milk solids fall to the bottom. Strain out the clear oil with a spoon —this is the ghee. For an equally delicious butter, substitute sage or other herbs for the lavender.

Lemongrass

Lemongrass is such an important herb in Southeast Asia that many homes there grow their own. Its celery-cilantro-ginger-citrusy floral aroma is what gives South Asian cuisines their distinct flavor, especially when it's combined with Kaffir lime leaves and galangal (a type of ginger), two other herbs used primarily in Thai, Malaysian, Cambodian, Vietnamese, and Indonesian cooking. Lemongrass is a tropical herb growing in bunches that look like long blades of grass. Because it's so fibrous, the grass can't be eaten unless finely chopped, but some people juice it as part of a detox program to help rebalance intestinal flora. Considered a superfood high in antioxidants and helpful for almost every ailment, it's used extensively in Ayurvedic medicine as a tea. Part of the citronella family, lemongrass's essential oils can also be used as an insect repellent. Lemongrass is also an herb you can add to lime and coconut and shake it all up.

In the Kitchen *To use lemongrass in a coconut soup or stew, remove the outer stalk and bruise the inner stalk to release its oils. Remove the stalks after cooking and before serving, or purée it finely into the dish. Fresh stalks can add a subtle Thai flavor to chicken noodle soup, curried squash, or pumpkin soup. Add a whole stalk to the water for poaching fish or steaming mussels. To grind it into a red or green curry paste with other spices, chop it into thin slices first. Make a marinade or stir-fry with chopped lemongrass, chiles, garlic, ginger, and shallots. Add it to yogurt with pineapple, mango, or papaya for an excellent smoothie. Grind it with garlic and peppercorns for a quick chicken rub, or add it to mashed root vegetables or green beans.*

REGIONAL STAR
Widely used in South Asian cooking, in the pork curries and chicken satays of Indonesia, the coconut milk soup and green and red curries of Thailand, and the spring rolls and soups of Vietnam.

HEALING POWER
anti-inflammatory, antiseptic, anticancer, antifungal, antiaging, antianxiety; high in vitamins and minerals; cleansing

WHERE TO BUY IT: Asian markets, specialty produce markets

HOW TO STORE IT: Fresh lemon-grass keeps for up to three weeks in the refrigerator. The flavor is better when frozen than dried. Plain lemon peel is preferable to dried lemongrass.

COMPLEMENTS

bamboo shoots
beef
carrots
chicken

chili paste
coconut milk
lemon zest
lime
lotus root
mushrooms
noodles
pineapple
poached fruit
potatoes
rice
sesame oil
shallots
soy sauce
teas
Thai basil
tomatoes
vinegar

PAIRS WELL WITH

cilantro
cinnamon
galangal
garlic
ginger
green onions
Kaffir lime leaf
tamarind
turmeric

FLAVOR PROFILE: *lemon, citrus, ginger, floral*

Thai Green Curry with Beef and Eggplant

Prep time: 20 minutes | Cook time: 20 minutes

Serves 4 to 6 *It's possible to buy premade green, yellow, or red Thai curry paste in the international section of the supermarket, but if you have a local Asian market where you can find Kaffir leaves, galangal (Thai ginger), and lemongrass, it's so much better to make your own.*

FOR THE GREEN CURRY PASTE
1 teaspoon coriander seeds
1 teaspoon cumin seeds
3 lemongrass stalks, white parts only chopped (remove outer part first)
3 shallots, sliced
1 tablespoon chopped galangal (substitute ginger if you can't find it)
4 Kaffir lime leaves, chopped (use lime rind if you can't find these)
3 garlic cloves
1 teaspoon chopped cilantro root (use the stems if you can't find the root)
1 tablespoon sugar
1 teaspoon salt
1 teaspoon shrimp paste (optional)
10 hot green chiles
2 tablespoons coconut or vegetable oil

FOR THE DISH
1 pound boneless steak
2 tablespoons coconut or vegetable oil
2½ cups coconut milk, divided

4 Kaffir lime leaves
1 Thai eggplant, cut into ¼-inch slices
2 tablespoons fish sauce
1 teaspoon sugar
1 bunch Thai basil
4 green chiles for garnish (optional)

TO MAKE THE GREEN CURRY PASTE

In a small pan over medium-high heat, dry roast the coriander and cumin seeds until toasted, 1 to 2 minutes.

In a mortar and pestle or food processor, grind the lemongrass, shallots, galangal, lime leaves, garlic, cilantro root, coriander seeds, cumin seeds, sugar, salt, shrimp paste (if using), and green chiles until smooth.

Add the oil and blend well.

TO MAKE THE DISH

Cut the beef into long, thin strips.

In a large frying pan over medium heat, heat the coconut oil. Add 3 large tablespoons of curry paste and fry until aromatic, about 2 minutes.

Slowly stir in 1¼ cups of coconut milk, and cook for about 5 minutes, until it looks like oily silk.

Add the beef, lime leaves, eggplant, fish sauce, and sugar, and cook for 3 to 4 minutes.

Stir in the remaining 1¼ cups of coconut milk, and cook until the meat and eggplant are tender, about 10 minutes.

Stir in the Thai basil and green chiles, and serve over jasmine rice.

TIP: Thailand creates dishes with green, red, and yellow curry paste. Green curry, like in this recipe, uses green ingredients like hot green chiles, cilantro, lemongrass, and Kaffir lime leaves. Basil and Kaffir lime leaves are often added as garnishes, and this is a traditional curry for beef and chicken. Red curry pastes generally have the same ingredients as green but use red chile peppers instead of green, and turmeric is often added for color. Yellow curries, which include beef and chicken, onions, potatoes, and carrots are often milder and usually have shallots, ginger, mustard powder, cinnamon, and brown sugar.

Marigold

Marigold is used to adulterate saffron, while its orange flowers have been used as a dye for fabrics and food. The petals are sometimes added to chicken feed to give a brighter golden color to the egg yolks. Also known as calendula, marigold is considered by gardeners one of the easiest flowers to grow. Since it repels insects, it's also a good companion plant for tomatoes. The flower petals are eaten rather than the leaves, which aren't very palatable. Marigold is high in antioxidants, and its anti-inflammatory proprieties make them a popular home remedy for minor cuts, scraps and burns. Emily Dickinson used to eat marigold petals, advising cutting off the leaves first because they gave a bitter taste.

In the Kitchen *Marigold flowers can be used fresh or dried as garnishes for soups and salads. The petals can color custards and puddings and be added to baked goods, butters, and soups. Sprinkle them into goat cheese, or cook them with rice or omelets for a cheap saffron substitute. The leaves taste great on a cucumber salad or in a sherry cream soup. You can candy the flowers or make a simple syrup from them. Add the petals to cheesecake, lemonade, or the tops of cupcakes, or substitute the flowers for squash blossoms and make fritters.*

REGIONAL STAR

The dried and ground petals of the French marigold are essential in Georgian cuisine. Also called Imeretian saffron, they are blended with cinnamon and cloves to make the spice mixture *khmeli suneli,* the Georgian version of India's garam masala. In the United States and Mexico, Mexican mint marigold can be substituted for tarragon. It pairs well with corn, beans, squash, and avocado and is drunk as a tea in Central America.

HEALING POWER

A tea made with marigold will help with intestinal disorders. Applied topically, it can help heal wounds.

WHERE TO BUY IT: Dried marigold petals can be found at some specialty grocery stores. Marigold powder is harder to find but is available online.

HOW TO STORE IT: Store dried marigold in a dry, airtight container. Use the fresh leaves of the Mexican mint marigold within a day or two.

COMPLEMENTS

avocado
baked goods
beans
berries
butters

cheesecake
corn
fruit
melon
salads
soups
squash
walnuts

PAIRS WELL WITH

cilantro
cinnamon
cloves
coriander

FLAVOR PROFILE: *Musky, bitter, citrusy, resin-like aroma*

Prep time: 5 minutes, plus time to pick the flowers

Serves 4 *Nothing could be more beautiful than a salad topped with flowers. Use any combination of flowers in this recipe. If the flowers are tiny, use them whole. Otherwise, if using those with flower heads like marigold and rose, just use the petals. You can buy packages of nasturtiums in the supermarket, but in the springtime, you should be able to find many edible flowers in your garden. Make sure you clearly identify the flowers you wish to use. Since flowers are so rich with their own flavors, a simple vinaigrette works best.*

FOR THE VINAIGRETTE
1 tablespoon red wine vinegar
1 tablespoon Dijon mustard
5 tablespoons extra-virgin olive oil
Salt
Freshly ground black pepper
Few drops orange flower water or rose water (if desired)

FOR THE SALAD
4 cups spring salad greens (arugula, watercress, baby kale, or whatever is available)
⅓ cup raspberries or blackberries (if desired)
1 to 2 cups any combination of the following flowers: borage, carnations, chrysanthemums, clover, cornflower, dandelion petals, elderberry, geranium, hibiscus, honeysuckle, jasmine, lavender, lilac, Mexican marigold (also called calendula), mustard, nasturtium, pansies, pea, radish, rose petals, safflower, squash, violets

In a small bowl, whisk together the vinegar, mustard, olive oil, salt, pepper, and orange flower water (if using).

In a salad bowl, toss the salad greens with the raspberries (if using) and flowers.

Toss the salad with the vinaigrette, arrange the flowers decoratively on top, and serve.

Prep time: 10 minutes | Cook time: 15 minutes

Serves 2 to 4 *These fried potatoes are topped with ground marigold, giving the potatoes an earthy, fragrant edge. If you can't find ground marigold, try a blend of fenugreek and paprika.*

1 pound potatoes
¾ to 1 cup cooking oil
Salt
1 tablespoon ground marigold
Few sprigs chopped cilantro, for garnish

Peel the potatoes and chop them into wedges or slices.

In a large saucepan over medium-high heat, heat the oil. Deep-fry the potatoes until tender and golden, about 15 minutes.

Using a slotted spoon, remove the potatoes to a paper towel–lined plate to drain.

Transfer the potatoes to a serving plate, season with salt, top with the marigold and cilantro sprigs, and serve.

TIP: Georgians traditionally fry these potatoes in the same oil in which a whole, uncut chicken has been fried and serve the whole mixture, family-style, with sliced onions.

Mint

Greek mythology calls mint the "herb of hospitality." Mint leaves were once strewn on the floor so that when guests walked over them, the bruised leaves would perfume the air. Since hearty mint grows year-round, it's a great addition to your garden or a pot on your deck. It likes partial shade and lots of water. If you place the pot on soil, mint's tenacious roots will break through the bottom of the pot and attempt to invade your garden. Since it's known as a bug repellent, some people keep pots of mint near the door to keep away flies, or even near cupboards or closets to repel mice. While the most common mints for cultivation are spearmint and peppermint, the mint family includes over 30 species. Other varieties include subtle hints of apple, chocolate (good for desserts), orange, banana, lemon, pineapple, and ginger, all of which contain the volatile oil menthol, giving mint its characteristic cooling sensation.

In the Kitchen *If you grow mint in your garden, harvest the leaves before they flower, since this is when the oils are strongest. Fresh mint is featured in drinks like the mojito and the mint julip, but it also adds depth to both sweet and savory dishes. Add it to minced lamb or to fresh green or fruit salads, or make a mint jelly for pork. Mint also makes a great dessert garnish for ice cream or chocolate cake.*

⁙ REGIONAL STAR

Make a sauce with a cup of yogurt, a cup of fresh mint leaves, salt, pepper, and two chopped cucumbers to accompany a leg of lamb for Middle Eastern flavor. Or substitute mint for tarragon in a French béarnaise for a sauce called Paloise to accompany fish or chicken. In Vietnam, mint is added to spring rolls and rice wraps. Indian cooks add it to chutneys, and Greeks use the dried version in the stuffing for grape leaves. In Morocco, mint is added to lentil stew.

✚ HEALING POWER

gallstones, irritable bowel syndrome, and is one of the oldest (and tastiest) medicinal herbs for indigestion

WHERE TO BUY IT: supermarket, online

HOW TO STORE IT: Use fresh leaves immediately after picking, or store in the refrigerator for up to three days. If the mint is still attached to the stems, place in a vase of water.

COMPLEMENTS

apples
balsamic vinegar
berries
cabbage
carrots
chickpeas

chiles
chocolate
coconut
cucumbers
dried fruits
eggplant
feta cheese
figs
grapefruit
lamb
lime
orange
peas
pine nuts
potatoes
shallots
spinach
tomatoes
yogurt
zucchini

PAIRS WELL WITH

---

basil
cardamom
chives
cilantro
dill
ginger

FLAVOR PROFILE: *fresh, aromatic, sweet flavor with cooling aftertaste*

Prep time: 20 minutes | Cook time: 5 minutes

Serves 4 *If you can find rice wraps at an Asian market, these wraps are a healthier and fresher version of the typically fried spring rolls. While you're at the market, pick up some rice vermicelli, a bottle of hoisin sauce (a type of plum sauce), and a bottle of fish sauce, which you will also need for this dish. These are great additions to any kitchen cabinet if you are planning to cook additional Asian dishes.*

FOR THE ROLLS
2 ounces rice vermicelli
4 tablespoons chopped fresh mint leaves
2 tablespoons chopped fresh cilantro
2 tablespoons chopped fresh basil (Thai basil is best if you can find it)
8 rice wrappers about 8 to 9 inches in diameter
8 large cooked shrimp or prawns, peeled, deveined, and halved

FOR THE DIPPING SAUCES
3 tablespoons hoisin sauce
2 teaspoons finely chopped roasted peanuts
1½ tablespoons fish sauce
¼ cup water
2 tablespoons freshly squeezed lime juice
1 garlic clove, minced
1 tablespoon sugar

TO MAKE THE ROLLS

Bring a medium pot of water to a boil over high heat. Add the vermicelli and boil for 3 to 5 minutes, until tender but not too soft.

Drain and rinse the vermicelli in a colander. Set aside on a plate.

In a medium bowl, stir together the mint, cilantro, and basil.

To soften a rice wrapper, fill a large bowl with warm water and dip the wrapper into it for a second.

Lay the wrapper flat and add 2 shrimp halves, a small handful of vermicelli, and an eighth of the fresh herb mixture, leaving about 2 inches on either side without any filling.

Fold the uncovered sides inward, and roll each wrap as snugly as possible.

Repeat with the remaining ingredients.

TO MAKE THE DIPPING SAUCES
In a small bowl, mix together the hoisin sauce and peanuts. In another small bowl, stir together the fish sauce, water, lime juice, garlic, and sugar.

Serve the rolls with the dipping sauces.

Berry Fruit Salad with Mint

Prep time: 10 minutes

Serves 6 to 8 *The fruit in this salad pairs especially nicely with mint. Don't be afraid to substitute whatever fruit is in season. Watermelon and mint go especially well together, too. Crème fraîche, or sour cream, dolloped on top, adds a decadent finish. This is a great salad to bring to a spring or summer picnic. Or purée the raspberries in a blender with some yogurt for a cold raspberry mint soup.*

1 small basket raspberries
1 small basket blueberries
1 small basket strawberries
2 mangos, peeled
Handful fresh mint, chopped, plus a few leaves for garnish
Dash balsamic vinegar
½ cup crème fraîche, sour cream, or yogurt

Wash the berries and pat them dry with a paper towel.

Chop the mangos into small pieces, about the size of the raspberries.

In a large bowl, toss together the raspberries, blueberries, strawberries, and mangos with the mint and balsamic vinegar.

Top with the crème fraîche, garnish with the mint leaves, and serve.

TIP: For a lower-calorie version, add a little vanilla and cinnamon to ½ cup of yogurt and substitute that for the crème fraîche. Or serve the fruit salad without any topping. The easiest way to cut a mango is to hold it, stem down, on a cutting board, and slice off the "cheeks," holding your knife about a quarter inch from the centerline. Repeat on the other side. What is left is mostly the seed. Slice a checkerboard pattern into each mango cheek, being careful not to cut through the skin on the other side. Then turn it inside out by pushing the skin up from underneath and, using your knife, scrape the mango chunks off the skin.

Oregano

Marjoram

The name *oregano* comes from the ancient Greek words *oros* and *ganos*, meaning *mountain joy*. In ancient Greece, couples were crowned with oregano as a symbol of happiness. Since oregano and marjoram are so similar in flavor (oregano is called wild marjoram in Europe), they are presented as one profile. Oregano and marjoram are both aromatic herbs of the mint family. Oregano can be substituted for marjoram (three parts marjoram for two parts oregano) and functions as a spice as well as an herb since its more pungent seeds are used in cooking, too. Medicinally, oregano is a superfood, containing more age-fighting antioxidants than blueberries, and rich in antiviral and antifungal properties. Inhaling the vapor of a few drops of oregano oil in boiling water can help cure respiratory illnesses, while oregano used topically can fight athlete's foot. Oregano seeds are also useful in alleviating menstrual cramps.

Oregano is easy to grow at home—being a perennial, it will come back next year.

In the Kitchen *Oregano (and marjoram) are primarily known in the United States as herbal additions to pizza and pasta sauces, but their aromatic flavors also complement eggs, salad dressings, and vegetables. You can purchase two varieties: Mediterranean, also called Greek or Turkish oregano, and Mexican. Though similar in taste, they originate from different plants. Mexican oregano is related to lemon verbena and has a stronger, more pungent flavor that works well in spicy dishes with chili powder and cumin. Mediterranean oregano is slightly sweeter and pairs best with milder dishes like fish, lamb, and salads. Oregano is a powerful enough herb that it can be added at the beginning of cooking. Oregano and marjoram are two of the few herbs that flavor food just as successfully dried as fresh.*

⁜ REGIONAL STAR

Add it to beans, stews, enchiladas, eggs, and corn in Mexican cooking and to bell peppers, chickpeas, grains, eggplant, pastas, feta cheese, salads, rice, potatoes, zucchini, and stuffed tomatoes in Mediterranean cuisine.

✚ HEALING POWER

fights parasitic infections, respiratory illnesses, menstrual cramps, viruses, food-borne illnesses, muscle pain, cancer, insects

WHERE TO BUY IT: supermarket, specialty grocery store, online

HOW TO STORE IT: fresh in a pot on your windowsill, in your garden, or dried in an airtight container

COMPLEMENTS

beans
chickpeas
corn
eggs
fish
kebabs
lamb
lemon
marinades
mushrooms
salad dressings
squash
tomatoes
zucchini

PAIRS WELL WITH

basil
cayenne
cumin
garlic
onions
salt

FLAVOR PROFILE: *aromatic, pungent, slightly sweet to slightly bitter*

Cold Gazpacho Soup with Fresh Oregano

Prep time: 10 minutes, plus 1 hour to chill

Serves 6 to 8 *This cold soup blends the herbaceous flavors of oregano and basil for a refreshing summer flavor. The key to this soup is finding the freshest and sweetest tomatoes. Served with toast, it's like the soup version of bruschetta.*

5 cups diced tomatoes
1 large cucumber, peeled and diced
1 medium red onion, chopped
¼ cup balsamic vinegar
¼ cup extra-virgin olive oil
4 garlic cloves, minced
2 tablespoons chopped fresh oregano
2 tablespoons chopped fresh basil
1 serrano chile, seeded
Salt
Freshly ground black pepper

In a large bowl, stir together the tomatoes, cucumber, red onion, balsamic vinegar, olive oil, garlic, oregano, basil, and the chile, seasoning with salt and pepper.

Using a food processor, pulse the ingredients in batches until they are soupy but chunky.

Transfer the soup to a bowl, cover, and refrigerate for an hour.

Serve with bread.

Roasted Corn with Oregano

Prep time: 5 minutes | Cook time: 10 minutes

Serves 4 *If you use fresh corn, you don't need to cook this very long, just until it's hot. This corn is roasted still in its husk, so the grassy flavors of the husk blend well with the herbaceous flavor of oregano. This corn can be wrapped in aluminum foil and roasted either in the oven or on a barbecue grill.*

**4 ears fresh corn
2 tablespoons butter
Salt
Freshly ground black pepper
2 tablespoons dried or finely chopped fresh oregano**

Preheat the oven to 425°F if roasting the corn in the oven. Otherwise, heat up the grill.

Pull the husks loose from the corn, but leave them attached to the stalk at the bottom.

Remove the silky threads from the inside.

Butter the corn by rubbing a chunk of butter all over it. Season with salt and pepper, and add oregano to each ear.

Wrap the corn back up in its husks.

If you are barbecuing them, you can lay them right on the grill and cook them until hot.

If you are roasting them in the oven, wrap them in aluminum foil and bake for about 15 minutes.

Serve hot. You can also serve these with chili powder or cayenne pepper.

TIP: You want to buy corn that has bright, fresh, plump kernels rather than dry, shriveled, or undeveloped ones. One way to test for this is to peel back the husks a little to check. But this will end up drying it out, leaving your annoyed grocer with a bin full of half-husked corn. Instead, look for corn with bright green husks that are free of any tiny green holes. These should be silky and slightly sticky, and you should be able to feel the plumpness of the kernels through the husk.

Parsley

The name *parsley* is derived from the Greek word meaning *rock celery* because it thrives in rocky areas, and the taste is reminiscent of celery. The Greeks initially cultivated it for its medicinal and ceremonial qualities, using it to adorn graves as well as crown their athletes. The Romans even believed it could help prevent intoxication. Valued for its breath-freshening character to help offset the smell of garlic, this herb can also neutralize both cigarette and charcoal grill smoke. A garnish that's often left uneaten, this herb is often the most nutritious food on a plate. A half cup of parsley contains 10 calories but provides half the daily recommended requirement of vitamin C and 550 percent the requirement of vitamin K, the so-called "overlooked" vitamin necessary for strong bones and blood clotting. Gardeners consider parsley an aid to the growth of tomatoes, and it helps bring out the tomato's flavor in the kitchen, as well.

In the Kitchen *Flat-leaf parsley, also called French or Italian parsley (not to be confused with Chinese parsley or cilantro), has the best flavor for cooking foods like omelets and stuffings. Or make a tartar sauce for fish with flat-leaf parsley, mayonnaise, shallots, capers, pickles, and green olives. The stems can be used, too, but are coarser in flavor. Curly parsley, the more decorative variety, is better for eating raw in garnishes, salad dressings, cold cuts, and mashed potatoes, and as a topping for chicken soup or mayonnaise.*

REGIONAL STAR

In Northern and Central Europe, where it was first cultivated in the sixteenth century, the parsley root is still used for cooking stews. Parsley is an essential herb in French cooking; the stems are used for bouquet garni (hearty herbs tied into a bundle and used for stocks) while the chopped leaves form the base of the *fines herbes* blend. Parsley is the main flavoring in Middle Eastern tabbouleh and in the Brazilian spice mixture *cheiro verde*, which translates as *green aroma*.

HEALING POWER

rich in vitamins A, C, K, iron, and beta carotene

WHERE TO BUY IT: supermarket

HOW TO STORE IT: Fresh parsley can last up to 4 to 5 days in the refrigerator. Dried parsley, having no flavor, is simply not recommended.

COMPLEMENTS

avocados
black pepper
cauliflower
chickpeas

cucumbers
eggplant
eggs
fish
garlic
lemon
lentils
mushrooms
mussels
olives
onions
parsnips
potatoes
rice
salt
stocks
tabbouleh
tomatoes

PAIRS WELL WITH

basil
bay leaf
chives
cumin
garlic
mint
oregano
pepper
rosemary
tarragon

FLAVOR PROFILE: *tangy and herbaceous with a light lemon-pepper note*

Tabbouleh

Prep time: 10 minutes, plus 1 hour to sit

Serves 6 to 8 *The combination of mint and parsley works well in this traditional Middle Eastern salad. For a heartier salad, add chickpeas. You can find bulgur wheat at most supermarkets, in specialty grocery stores, or online.*

1½ cups boiling water
1 cup bulgur wheat
Juice of 2 lemons (¼ cup)
¼ cup extra-virgin olive oil
3 teaspoons salt, divided
1 cup minced green onions
1 bunch chopped fresh flat-leaf parsley (1 cup)
1 bunch chopped fresh mint (1 cup)
1 medium cucumber, peeled, seeded, and diced
2 cups finely chopped tomatoes
1 (8-ounce) can chickpeas (optional)
Freshly ground black pepper

In a large bowl, pour the boiling water over the bulgur.

Add the lemon juice, olive oil, and 1½ teaspoons of salt, and stir.

Allow the mixture to sit at room temperature for an hour.

Mix in the green onions, parsley, mint, cucumber, tomatoes, and chickpeas (if using), and season with the remaining 1½ teaspoons of salt and the pepper.

Serve or refrigerate. The tabbouleh's flavors will blend together better if allowed to sit for a couple of hours.

Parsley, White Wine, Garlic, and Steamed Mussels

Prep time: 5 minutes | Cook time: 10 minutes

Serves 6 to 8 *Serve this dish with a loaf of good-quality crusty bread to sop up the juices, a bottle of Tabasco sauce, and the rest of the wine, or an additional bottle. Alternatively, you can serve the mussels over pasta that has been sprinkled with salt, pepper, olive oil, and some chopped parsley.*

- **3¼ to 4 pounds mussels**
- **2 tablespoons extra-virgin olive oil**
- **2 tablespoons butter**
- **6 to 8 medium garlic cloves, finely chopped**
- **4 shallots, minced**
- **2 cups dry white wine**
- **1 cup chopped fresh flat-leaf parsley, divided**
- **1 loaf hot, crusty bread**

Rinse the mussels under cold water, scrubbing them with a stiff brush to remove any grit. Discard any that are broken or open.

In a large pot with a lid over medium heat, heat the olive oil and butter.

Add the garlic and shallots and cook until soft, 3 to 5 minutes.

Add the mussels, wine, and ¾ cup of parsley.

Increase the heat to high and cover the pan.

After 2 minutes, stir with a large spoon.

Cover and cook for another 3 to 5 minutes, until the mussels have opened.

Add the remaining ¼ cup of parsley, and serve the mussels in bowls with the broth, and the loaf of bread on the table.

TIP: When selecting mussels, choose those that smell fresh like the ocean but not fishy. Make sure the shells are closed, or that they close immediately when lightly tapped. Keep them in an open plastic bag (without air, they will suffocate) on a bed of ice in the refrigerator, and use them within one day. Just before cooking, check to see if any have opened, and discard those.

Rosemary

It's hard not to associate the herb rosemary with Shakespeare's Ophelia and her memorable line, "There's rosemary. That's for remembrance." At the time, it was indeed believed that rosemary could improve memory. And even recently it's been used during war memorials. The name *rosemary* is derived from the Latin, meaning *dew of the sea*, though mythically its purple flowers are associated with the Virgin Mary's blue shawl, which she supposedly set on top of the bush to dry, hence the name Rose of Mary. Thriving during the English Tudor period, rosemary was a symbol of fidelity, and a bride would give a sprig of it to her groom. In the ninth century, Charlemagne grew rosemary on his ranch in Spain. If you live in at least a partially sunny climate, you probably have some growing in your neighborhood, too. You can recognize this shrub by its short needles, tiny purple flowers, and strong, bitter pine aroma.

In the Kitchen Rosemary's flavor is slightly aggressive and can take over any dish if too much is added, so use with caution. The young stems can be used to flavor olive oils, and the more mature stems can be used to skewer meat for kebabs. Rosemary is excellent in a lamb marinade, imparting a smoky, almost mustardy flavor to the meat when roasted. It's also wonderful with garlic, roasted potatoes, and other root vegetables. Avoid chopping rosemary when adding it to soups because it can end up looking like little twigs. Instead, try stirring your soup with a branch or adding a sprig to a broth or sauce and removing it before serving.

REGIONAL STAR

Rosemary is one of the herbs in the French spice mixture herbes de Provence, though the Italians are more enthused about the herb than the French, scattering it through almost all their meat dishes, breads, and pasta sauces. In other Mediterranean cuisines, it's often cooked with root vegetables.

HEALING POWER

Good source of iron, calcium, and vitamin B_6. Rich in antioxidants and anti-inflammatory compounds. Has been used to boost the immune system, improve optical health, and increase memory and concentration. It also may help prevent brain aging.

WHERE TO BUY IT: supermarket, and most likely a bush in your neighborhood

HOW TO STORE IT: in the refrigerator, or in a glass of water for up to about five days

COMPLEMENTS

**balsamic vinegar
chicken**

corn
crackers
eggs
feta
figs
goat cheese
honey
lamb
lemon
mushrooms
olives
polenta
pork
potatoes
rabbit
squash
sweet potatoes

PAIRS WELL WITH

bay leaf
garlic
lavender
mint
oregano
parsley
sage
salt
thyme

FLAVOR PROFILE: *woody, astringent, with notes of bitter pepper, sage, and pine*

Prep time: 5 minutes | Cook time: 45 minutes

Serves 4 to 6 *This recipe is from San Francisco's Sociale restaurant chef Tia Harrison. She serves it topped with sautéed pork belly, but these grits are also delicious on their own. She recommends using grits from Anson Mills in South Carolina.*

3 cups water
Salt
1 cup stone-ground grits
1 bunch chopped fresh rosemary
1 cup heavy cream
2 cups freshly grated Parmesan cheese

In a medium saucepan over high heat, bring the water to a boil. Season with salt and add the grits.

Reduce the heat to low and cook, stirring often, for about 30 minutes.

Add the rosemary, cream, and Parmesan cheese, and season with additional salt.

Stir and simmer on low for another 15 minutes, and serve.

Rosemary Chuffed Potatoes

Prep time: 15 minutes | Cook time: 40 minutes

Serves 4 to 6 *Some believe that rosemary was invented especially for these potatoes. The secret to the golden crust on these potatoes is boiling them before baking, and then "chuffing" them, as explained in the instructions.*

6 to 8 russet potatoes, peeled and cut into ¾-inch cubes
¼ to ⅓ cup extra-virgin olive oil
Sea salt
⅓ cup chopped fresh rosemary, plus extra sprigs
6 garlic cloves, roughly chopped

Preheat the oven to 450°F.

In a large pot filled with water over high heat, boil the potatoes until you can stick a fork in them, but they are still somewhat firm and not mushy, about 10 minutes.

Drain the potatoes in a colander; then gently shake them up and down in the colander so that the potatoes develop a thin coating of softened potato around the outside.

Pour them in a single layer onto a baking sheet.

Drizzle the olive oil over them, and stir the potatoes around with your hand so that all of the potato is lightly coated.

Add the salt, rosemary, rosemary sprigs, and garlic, being sure to coat all the potatoes thoroughly with rosemary.

Bake in the oven until golden brown, 20 to 30 minutes.

Serve hot with a salt shaker on the table.

Sage

As the old rhyme goes, "He who drinks sage in May, shall live for aye." Sage is associated with wizened ones because drinking sage tea was believed to improve memory. Interestingly, sage has recently been credited with helping prevent Alzheimer's disease. It is also useful for menstrual problems, digestive difficulties, and oral health and can be used as an antiseptic, a sore throat tonic, and a nerve calmer; however, since medicinal qualities of the herb depend on the species of sage, self-treatment is not recommended. Because of its aromatic quality, monks used to plant sage in monastery gardens—its large, velvety leaves were also quite lovely compared to several of the more weedy-looking herbs. Beginning in the 1660s, a royal herb strewer was appointed to strew mixtures of sage, lavender, and roses through the streets to relieve royal noses of the scents of the sewer. The herb is still sacred among many Native American traditions as a cleansing herb.

In the Kitchen *Western cooks are probably most familiar with sage in an onion-sage Thanksgiving stuffing, but this versatile herb can be used more often than once a year. It adds flavor to sausages and other fatty meats and is useful for mellowing the wildness of gamey meat—try it minced into lamb or moose burgers. Substitute it for basil in pesto; stuff it into baked tomatoes with Parmesan cheese or baked potatoes with butter and parsley; or add it to white beans with garlic. A strongly flavored herb, sage is best when it's the featured flavor of a dish, such as in pasta or ravioli with browned butter and pumpkin or squash.*

REGIONAL STAR

Used in some specialty Italian dishes, sage is one of the few herbs not usually used in French cooking. British cooks use sage for fatty meats like goose and duck, while Italians include it in the classic veal dish saltimbocca.

HEALING POWER

Helps with digestion, oral health, menstrual health, and easing anxiety and is possibly a preventive for Alzheimer's.

WHERE TO BUY IT: supermarket

HOW TO STORE IT: Dried sage is more potent than fresh; since the fresh is already very potent, avoid the dried form in cooking. Fresh sage is best as soon as it's picked. It can stay in the refrigerator, in a damp towel, for a few days.

COMPLEMENTS

apples
artichokes
brown butter
butternut squash

chestnuts
corn
lemon
pasta
pine nuts
pinto beans
pumpkin
ricotta
rutabaga
stuffings
tomatoes
vinegar
walnuts

PAIRS WELL WITH

---

bay leaf
caraway
fennel
garlic
ginger
onion
rosemary
savory
thyme

FLAVOR PROFILE: *bitter and sweet with notes of lemon and eucalyptus*

Browned Butter–Sage Sauce with Tagliatelle and Pumpkin

Prep time: 10 minutes | Cook time: 30 minutes

Serves 4 *This autumn dish is perfect when pumpkins are in season. It's a variation of the scrumptious pumpkin ravioli with sage butter, only easier. Instead of making ravioli, this recipe just tosses tagliatelle noodles with chunks of pumpkin. If you like, you can substitute butternut squash for the pumpkin.*

1 pound pumpkin or butternut squash
2 tablespoons extra-virgin olive oil
8 tablespoons butter, divided
3 tablespoons minced shallots
Salt
Freshly ground black pepper
Pinch ground nutmeg
½ cup chicken or vegetable stock
12 fresh sage leaves
16 ounces fresh or dried tagliatelle noodles
4 ounces Parmesan cheese, grated

Peel the pumpkin, remove the skin and the hard layer beneath it, and cut the flesh into ½-inch chunks.

In a medium saucepan over medium-high heat, heat the olive oil and 2 tablespoons of butter. Fry the shallots until soft.

Add the pumpkin and continue to cook for 2 to 3 minutes. Season with salt, pepper, and nutmeg, and add the stock.

Bring to a boil, cover, and simmer for about 10 minutes, until the pumpkin is tender.

In a large saucepan over medium heat, melt the remaining 6 tablespoons of butter.

Add the sage, season with a little salt, and cook until the butter begins to brown, 10 to 15 minutes. Make sure the butter browns but doesn't burn. The leaves should be crisp. Remove from the heat.

Meanwhile, bring a large pot of boiling water to a boil over high heat. Cook the tagliatelle. Allow 3 to 4 minutes for fresh pasta or about 12 minutes for dried.

When the pasta is tender but not too soft, drain and turn onto a warmed dish. Season with salt and pepper.

Divide the pasta among 4 plates. For each plate add one-quarter of the pumpkin mixture in the middle, spoon one-quarter of the sage butter over it, and top with one-quarter of the deep-fried sage leaves.

Sprinkle an ounce of Parmesan cheese over each plate, and serve.

TIP: If you can find butternut squash or pumpkin ravioli at a specialty grocery store, just make the sage butter and pour it over the ravioli.

Savory

Savory comes in 30 varieties, but only 2 have culinary value: summer and winter. Summer savory is a delicate annual herb grown only in summer, though it can be found in its dry form throughout the year. It has delicate, light green leaves and is fragrantly reminiscent of thyme and marjoram. Winter savory, grown over the winter, has darker green leaves and a more intense peppery flavor with a pine-like aftertaste. Savory is one of the herbs that make up the French herbal blend herbes de Provence (the others being marjoram, oregano, rosemary, and thyme), and its essential oils, used in making bitters and vermouth, are also considered medicinal. Savory was originally imported to North America for its antiseptic and digestive properties—or perhaps for its bedroom benefits. French herbalists suggested using savory as an aphrodisiac. Interestingly, summer savory is purported to increase the sex drive, while winter savory is said to decrease it.

In the Kitchen *Summer and winter savory naturally complement the produce in season alongside them. Try summer savory with summer squash, fresh fava or green beans, and artichoke hearts; and winter savory with dried beans and a bay leaf. Summer savory is best used in its fresh form as a condiment or with garlic and lemon for a fish marinade. Winter savory is better for long-stewed dishes, though many prefer the summer version for the same purpose, if it's in season. In any form, savory works well as a seasoning for meats —traditionally, it's ground into pork and sausages. Summer savory complements, rather than overpowers, so you can use it more generously than the winter variety.*

⁂ REGIONAL STAR

Summer savory is used extensively in Canada, where it grows best. In Bulgaria, summer savory is a condiment next to salt and paprika on the table. In Romania, savory is used in stuffed cabbage rolls, while in the Mediterranean, it's used in lamb and rabbit stews and sheep cheese.

✚ HEALING POWER

rich in potassium, iron, calcium, magnesium, manganese, zinc, and selenium and has antibacterial and antiseptic qualities

WHERE TO BUY IT: Savory is often not available in supermarkets, so it's best to purchase the plants from nurseries or grow your own from seed.

HOW TO STORE IT: Summer savory keeps for about a week in the refrigerator, winter savory a little longer. It also freezes well.

COMPLEMENTS

beans
beets

cauliflower
eggs
fatty meats
fresh cheeses
peas
potatoes
poultry
squash
stocks
tomatoes
vinegars

PAIRS WELL WITH

asparagus
basil
bay leaf
garlic
marjoram
mint
oregano
paprika
parsley
rosemary
rutabagas
sage
tarragon

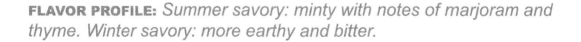

FLAVOR PROFILE: *Summer savory: minty with notes of marjoram and thyme. Winter savory: more earthy and bitter.*

Goose with Summer Savory Stuffing

Prep time: 30 minutes | Cook time: 3 to 4 hours

Serves 10 to 12 *Summer and winter savory can replace traditional sage in stuffing. Savory pairs especially well with fatty meat like goose, but if you don't have a goose on hand, you could use this stuffing for a chicken or turkey, too. This makes enough stuffing for an 11-pound goose. If you are using it with chicken, find the biggest chicken you can, and cut the recipe in half.*

1 pound dense bread, cut into ¾-inch cubes
1 (10- to 12-pound) goose
1 lemon, halved
1½ teaspoons salt, divided
1½ teaspoons freshly ground black pepper, divided
1 bunch fresh summer savory, chopped, a few sprigs left whole (if you don't have fresh summer savory, use dried, but less of it, or use less winter savory)
¼ cup butter
2 onions, chopped
2 celery stalks, chopped
1 leek
6 garlic cloves, minced
1 tablespoon fresh oregano or 1 teaspoon dried
1 tablespoon fresh thyme
1½ cups chicken broth, divided
1 egg

Preheat the oven to 350°F.

Toast the bread cubes on a baking sheet for 10 to 15 minutes.

Increase the oven heat to 400°F.

Rub the goose inside and out with the lemon, and then sprinkle it with ½ teaspoon each of salt and pepper.

Loosen the skin around the goose and tuck fresh savory sprigs underneath.

In a large frying pan over medium heat, melt the butter and sauté the onions, celery, and leek until soft, 5 to 10 minutes. Add the garlic and cook an additional minute.

In a large bowl, mix the bread cubes and onion mixture. Add the remaining teaspoon each of salt and pepper, the oregano and thyme, 1 cup of the broth, and the egg. Toss gently.

Stuff the bird and place it on a roasting pan.

Put the remaining stuffing in a baking dish and sprinkle it with the remaining ½ cup of broth. Use less liquid if there is less stuffing left.

Bake the goose breast-side up and uncovered for 30 minutes.

Reduce the heat to 350°F, cover the goose, and bake for an additional 2½ to 3 hours, until tender.

Bake the additional stuffing, covered, for 30 minutes.

Uncover the goose and bake for an additional 10 minutes, until brown.

Remove the goose from the oven, cover, and let sit for 15 to 20 minutes.

Carve and serve.

Scented Geranium

It might come as a surprise that scented geranium, a plant usually associated with the French perfume industry, has so many uses in the kitchen. The flowers of scented geraniums are smaller than the regular geraniums you see on French balconies, but the scent is so potent that they were once grown in huge quantities for manufacturing perfume. Scented geraniums first became popular during the Victorian era for scenting teas, cakes, wines, and teas, and perhaps in the parlor game "Identify that scent." Since then, they've fallen a little out of fashion, but the huge varieties of scents from over 200 different varieties of geraniums can still reproduce the scents from almost all the spices in your cupboard, including cinnamon, clove, nutmeg, and even chocolate. Other aromas include apple, strawberry, apricot, lemon, mint, and rose. These aromatics offer wide varieties and wild possibilities for baking experimentation.

In the Kitchen *The best scented geraniums for culinary use are lemon, mint, and rose. Though you don't necessarily want to eat the leaves, if they are dry and clean, you can stack them in sugar to perfume it for later use in cakes or frostings. The leaves can be added to jams and jellies or sugar syrups or used to garnish lemonade to impart a floral aroma. To make custards, puddings, or ice cream, bruise the leaves in the hot cream or milk, cool, and then strain. Or add the leaves to sweet vinegars with lemon verbena, basil, and mint. The leaves can be candied and added to cakes or added to mojitos or mint juleps. Martha Stewart arranges them on top of parchment paper in the baking pan in which she pours the batter for pound cake. Baked that way, they will add a delicate floral note to any cake.*

❋ REGIONAL STAR
Victorian England and North America

✚ HEALING POWER
A tea made from the leaves has the same calming effect as chamomile.

WHERE TO BUY IT: nurseries in the spring. Worth growing at home, as they flourish easily. You can grow them in pots, and bring them inside when it gets cold.

HOW TO STORE IT: Pick flowers just before using. Leaves will keep in the refrigerator for five days.

COMPLEMENTS

berries
cakes
custards
fruit

lemon
pancakes
puddings
sugar
tea
wine

PAIRS WELL WITH

---

basil
mint

FLAVOR PROFILE: *aromas including clove, nutmeg, apple, cinnamon, lemon, rose, mint, chocolate mint*

Prep time: 1 hour, plus 1 day to 2 weeks to sit in the sun

Makes 1 quart *Most flower waters require a steam distillation process that is beyond the abilities of this guide to describe, but you can make your own flower waters at home that are not quite as potent, though still work, using a simpler method. Because scented geranium's leaves are so strong, it infuses water more easily than most other blossoms. If you prefer, however, you can also use orange blossoms, rose petals, jasmine blossoms, or lavender flowers.*

1 cup fresh scented geranium leaves (choose your favorite scent)
Distilled water

Thoroughly wash the leaves in cold water.

Bruise the leaves by gently rolling them in your hands, and place them in a quart-size glass jar with a lid.

Fill the jar with the distilled water.

Keep the jar in the sun for 1 day to 2 weeks. Since geranium leaves are so fragrant, they don't require a long time. Other blossoms will require a longer waiting time.

Strain the geranium water into a separate, clean container, and store in the refrigerator.

TIP: If you are using jasmine blossoms, lavender flowers, rose petals, or orange blossoms, pound them in a mortar first. Add the blossoms to cakes, puddings, ice cream, whipped cream, fruit desserts, honey, or sparkling water. Another way to impart the flavor of blossoms to your dishes is to simply add the blossoms at the end of cooking.

Prep time: 20 minutes | Cook time: 5 to 7 minutes | Total time: 27 minutes, plus overnight to chill

Serves 8 *This exceedingly simple pie is so delicious, you'll want to make it for every special occasion. The geranium leaves add an especially aromatic depth to the flavors of lemon and vanilla.*

1 (12-ounce) box vanilla wafers
4 tablespoons melted butter
1 teaspoon lemon geranium leaves (finely chopped)
1 (14-ounce) can sweetened condensed milk
Zest of 1 lemon
½ cup freshly squeezed lemon juice
1 cup heavy whipping cream
3 tablespoons sugar
1 teaspoon vanilla

Preheat the oven to 400°F.

Count out enough vanilla wafers to line the edges of a pie pan and set aside.

Leave about one-quarter of the wafers in the box to eat later, and crush the rest of them in a food processor, so that they are crumbly but not powdery. Alternatively, you can put them in a plastic bag and crush them with a rolling pin.

In a small bowl, stir together the melted butter with the crushed wafers and lemon geranium leaves.

Pat the mixture into the bottom of the pie pan.

Line the sides of the pie pan with the reserved whole wafers, cutting one in half if necessary to make them fit all around.

Bake for 5 to 7 minutes until golden, and allow to cool.

In a small bowl, beat the sweetened condensed milk with the lemon zest and lemon juice.

Pour the lemon mixture into the crust.

Whip the cream until soft peaks form; then whip in the sugar and vanilla.

Layer the whipped cream over the lemon mixture.

Chill in the refrigerator overnight.

Serve cold.

Tarragon

If you haven't developed a slight crush on tarragon, it could be that you have been using the dried or the tougher, less aromatic Russian version rather than the French variety. French tarragon is harder to grow; its roots must be grafted, rather than grown from seed. If you are lucky enough to find it at a nursery, keep a pot of it on your windowsill; it likes the sun, and unlike many other windowsill herbs, not a lot of water. Mexican tarragon, sometimes called Mexican mint marigold, is a better substitute for French tarragon than the more hearty Russian variety. Tarragon, parsley, chives, and chervil make up the four herbs of the classic French *fines herbes*. Unlike basil, thyme, rosemary, and bay leaf, these more delicate herbs lose their flavors after too much cooking and are therefore usually added at the end. Infuse flavor to vinegars or oils with tarragon by bruising the leaves before adding them.

In the Kitchen *Lay whole tarragon stems under and inside fish. Try it in a chicken stew with white wine, or add it to corn chowder. Add it to bacon or mac and cheese, mix it with chives in an herb omelet, or even sprinkle it on top of strawberries. Make a creamy tarragon salad dressing to top a seafood salad, or add it in moderation to a green salad. Add it to sautéed carrots, or substitute it for chives in baked potatoes. Mix it with mustard to braise lamb or chicken. Heat somewhat diminishes the flavor of the fresh herb, so add it at the end of cooking or as a garnish.*

❊ REGIONAL STAR

Throughout the former Soviet countries, a fizzy drink called tarragon soda was, and still is, a popular substitute for lemonade. In French cooking, tarragon is a crucial component to béarnaise sauce, a sauce typically paired with steak and a cousin to the classic hollandaise sauce.

✛ HEALING POWER

high in iron, potassium, vitamins, and antioxidants. Like cloves, tarragon contains eugenol, which is useful as a toothache remedy and for easing anxiety.

WHERE TO BUY IT: supermarket, but grow your own if you can find the French variety

HOW TO STORE IT: Fresh sprigs will keep for about five days.

COMPLEMENTS

apples
artichokes
asparagus
beets
bitter greens

capers
carrots
cauliflower
corn
eggs
fish
lime
mustard
parsley
pasta
potatoes
poultry
shallots
spinach
stuffing
tomatoes
vinegar

PAIRS WELL WITH

bay leaf
celery seeds
chervil
chives
dill
garlic
marjoram
mustard
paprika
pepper

FLAVOR PROFILE: *slight licorice tones and notes of lemon, mint, and basil*

Prep time: 5 minutes | Cook time: 10 minutes

Serves 6 to 8 *It seems important to include a recipe for the French sauce that makes tarragon so beloved. Béarnaise sauce is similar to hollandaise sauce but flavored with tarragon, pepper, and shallots rather than lemon, and typically poured over steak. It's also great with ham. Try pouring it over asparagus doused with olive oil, salt, and pepper, and then grilled or baked in the oven at 400° for about 12 minutes. Roasting asparagus in this way gives it a similar meaty flavor to steak. This recipe makes enough sauce for both asparagus and steak.*

⅛ **cup white wine vinegar**
⅛ **cup white wine**
2 tablespoons minced shallot
7 black peppercorns, ground
⅓ **cup fresh minced tarragon, divided**
1 tablespoon freshly squeezed lemon juice
4 teaspoons water
½ **teaspoon salt, plus more for seasoning**
3 large egg yolks
1 cup melted butter

In a small saucepan over medium heat, cook down the vinegar, wine, shallots, pepper, and half of the tarragon (about 2½ tablespoons) until it is reduced by half.

In a medium bowl, whisk the lemon juice, water, and salt together.

Strain the vinegar mixture into the lemon juice. Set aside.

Whisk the egg yolks into the vinegar mixture, and then place the bowl over a pot of simmering water and whisk constantly. (This is the most fragile part because if the eggs harden, you will have to start over.)

When the mixture has nearly doubled in size and starts to foam, start pouring in the melted butter. The sauce should start to become smooth and silky.

After all the butter is incorporated, whisk in the remaining tarragon (about 2½ tablespoons) and season with salt.

Serve immediately.

TIP: If you don't have any white wine, you can substitute vinegar, and if you don't have white wine vinegar, apple cider vinegar will do. As long as you don't get distracted while whisking in the butter, you won't have a problem making this sauce. The hardest part is timing it so that you can serve it hot. As a variation, try substituting sage for the tarragon.

Tarragon and Goat Cheese Omelet

Prep time: 5 minutes | Cook time: 10 minutes

Serves 2 to 3 *You can add two more of the other French fine herbs, chervil and parsley, but tarragon is really all you need since tarragon and goat cheese complement each other so well. While this dish is simple to prepare, the fresh herbs and goat cheese make breakfast feel like a special occasion.*

6 eggs
2 tablespoons milk or cream
1 teaspoon freshly ground black pepper, plus more for serving
2 tablespoons butter
5 sprigs tarragon, finely chopped
5 sprigs chives, finely chopped
3 ounces goat cheese, crumbled
Salt

Preheat the oven to 450°F.

In a medium bowl, whisk the eggs with the cream and pepper until slightly foamy.

In a medium ovenproof pan over medium-high heat, melt the butter.

When the butter is sizzling, pour in the egg mixture.

Add the tarragon, chives, and goat cheese, and swirl the mixture around a little until the eggs set, about 2 minutes.

Put the eggs in the oven for a minute, or until the top is set. If you prefer not to use the oven, flip half of the omelet over the other like a taco and cook, covered, until the inside is set.

Serve with salt and pepper.

TIP: To avoid the brown spots of burnt butter in your omelet, clarify the butter first by simmering it over low heat. When all the butter has melted and the white milk solids sink to the bottom, spoon out the clear oil on top. This oil can withstand a high heat.

Thyme

When the Greeks said that someone "smelled of thyme," they meant he or she was extremely elegant and fashionable. The active volatile chemical thymol gives thyme its characteristic aroma, and, among other uses, is the active ingredient in Listerine. (Perhaps smelling like mouthwash was very stylish at the time.) In the Middle Ages, perhaps because it grew so valiantly on the hot, arid hillsides of the Mediterranean, thyme was associated with courage, and girls would give a sprig to their favorite knight. These days, thyme is mostly used in North America to flavor clam chowder and marinate pork and game. Lemon thyme, with its citrusy note, is better for poultry and seafood, while the more common thyme is better for meat. Middle Eastern chefs use thyme in their spice mixture za'atar, which is also the name for one of the varieties of thyme that grows there. Other varieties include caraway thyme, creeping thyme, and orange-scented thyme.

In the Kitchen *Unlike most herbs, thyme retains its flavor even after a long, slow cooking time. Thyme is a helpmate to other herbs and doesn't have to take center stage. It's particularly good in wine- or beer-based sauces or in a brandy cream sauce. Try it in a salad dressing or a fish or chicken marinade combined with garlic, lemon, and olive oil, or add it to braised artichokes. For the wild mushroom hunter lucky enough to bring home a bag of chanterelles, mushrooms sautéed in butter, salt, pepper, and a little thyme are the crowning glory of the treasure hunt. Thyme also perks up beets and other root vegetables, and the flavors of thyme, garlic, wine, onion, and olive oil in a tomato sauce complement each other beautifully.*

REGIONAL STAR

The dried herb is used in the gumbos and jambalayas of Creole and Cajun cooking. It can also be found in almost every French stock and Spanish stew, while in Latin America, thyme is usually combined with chiles.

HEALING POWER

Can help prevent acne and high blood pressure. Contains antimicrobial properties that can help cure yeast infections and acute chest infections. Boosts immunity and enhances feelings of well-being.

WHERE TO BUY IT: supermarket

HOW TO STORE IT: up to a week in the refrigerator for fresh thyme; six months for dried thyme

COMPLEMENTS

artichokes
beans
Brussels sprouts

343

corn
eggplant
jambalayas
lemon
marinades
mushrooms
olive oil
onions
potatoes
roasted chicken
seafood
stews
stocks
stuffings

PAIRS WELL WITH

basil
bay leaf
chives
fennel
mustard
parsley
sesame seeds
sumac

FLAVOR PROFILE: *hints of clove, mint, lemon, and camphor*

Thyme-Stuffed Baked Tomatoes

Prep time: 15 minutes | Cook time: 35 minutes

Serves 4 *A seventeenth-century recipe including thyme claimed that those who ate the dish would be able to see fairies. This recipe cannot make the same claim, but you could give it a try. The following ingredients, which taste so delicious in a tomato sauce, also go well inside a simple tomato.*

4 beefsteak tomatoes
Salt
2 tablespoons extra-virgin olive oil, plus more for drizzling
1 onion, finely chopped
2 garlic cloves, minced
½ cup bread crumbs
1 tablespoon chopped fresh thyme
2 tablespoons chopped fresh flat-leaf parsley
2 ounces Parmesan cheese, freshly grated
Freshly ground black pepper

Preheat the oven to 350°F.

Cut the tomatoes in half. Using a spoon, gently scrape out the flesh, being careful not to puncture the tomato skin.

Lightly salt the tomato.

In a large pan over medium heat, heat the oil and sauté the onion. When soft and translucent, add the garlic and bread crumbs, and sauté for a few minutes more.

Remove from the heat; stir in the thyme, parsley, and Parmesan, and season with pepper.

Place the tomatoes in a buttered baking dish and fill them with the herbal bread crumb mixture. Drizzle a little olive oil on top.

Bake for 25 to 30 minutes.

Serve warm.

Thyme, Caper, and Lemon–Marinated Fish

Prep time: 5 minutes, plus 1 to 24 hours to marinate | Cook time: 10 to 15 minutes

Serves 2 to 3 *Capers, lemon, and thyme seem to have been created for each other, and you'll find this easy marinade works with almost any white fish you choose. This recipe makes enough for two pounds of fish fillets.*

2 tablespoons freshly squeezed lemon juice, plus thin lemon slices for garnish
3 tablespoons white wine
2 tablespoons extra-virgin olive oil
3 tablespoons finely chopped shallots
2 tablespoons capers, plus 1 tablespoon of the juice
12 sprigs fresh lemon thyme, divided
2 pounds white fish fillets (bass, trout, snapper, cod, or halibut)
Salt
Freshly ground black pepper

In the baking dish you will use for the fish, beat together the lemon juice, wine, and olive oil.

Add the shallots, capers, caper juice, and most of the thyme.

In the baking dish, slather the marinade all over the fish, including the inside.

Tuck the remaining thyme sprigs inside the fish.

Lay the lemon slices on top of the fish.

Cover and refrigerate for at least an hour but not more than 24 hours.

On the grill or in a grill pan on the stove, grill the fish for 15 minutes, until flaky.

Season with salt and pepper, and serve.

TIP: Try substituting lime for the lemon.

Watercress

A breath freshener and palate cleanser, watercress gets its name from growing in waterways. It is sometimes difficult to find in the supermarket because, once picked, it lasts only one or two days. You can generally find it during the spring, though. One of the oldest herbs consumed by humans, watercress also ranks as one of the most nutritious and is higher in fiber, protein, potassium, and vitamins A, B_{12}, and D than chard, spinach, kale, and Brussels sprouts. Consider it an appropriate herb for a "spring cleaning" of the blood. Irish monks reported surviving on only watercress and bread. In the nineteenth century, watercress, called poor man's bread, was rolled up and eaten as a sandwich. (Fast food was a lot healthier then.) Since it grows so prodigiously, it's easy to find near streams. If you are lucky enough to find it growing wild, however, be sure to soak it well in salt water, since the water it grows in may contain bacteria.

In the Kitchen *Watercress can be stir-fried quickly with garlic, miso, and sesame oil, but it is best eaten raw. Add it to a sandwich or a salad with ingredients like balsamic vinegar and strawberries, avocado and grapefruit, or cucumber, red onion, and mint. Have it on toast with avocado, asparagus, hummus, or a poached egg. Try it in potato salad with beets and eggs, or add it to a cream-based soup. Watercress is sometimes blended into red pepper mayonnaise as an accompaniment to fish stew. Nasturtium leaves, part of the family of cress, can also be eaten but are sadly underused. Their bright, colorful flowers can be strewn on top of salads for a beautifully festive-looking dish.*

REGIONAL STAR

The French make a potato soup with watercress called *potage au cresson.* Italians sometimes add watercress to minestrone, and Chinese chefs add it to egg drop soup.

HEALING POWER

antioxidant, diuretic, stimulant, and digestive aid

WHERE TO BUY IT: in bunches by itself at the supermarket, though it's usually mixed with salad greens. It's also an easy herb to grow from seed.

HOW TO STORE IT: in the refrigerator for four to five days

COMPLEMENTS

avocado
beets
blue and Cheddar cheese
carrots
eggs
grapefruit

lemon
mayonnaise
mushrooms
olives
peaches
pears
pistachios
pomegranates
radicchio
sandwiches
shallots
tomatoes
vinegar
walnuts
yogurt

PAIRS WELL WITH

dill
garlic
ginger
parsley
pepper
sesame seeds
thyme

FLAVOR PROFILE: *mild flavor of spring to hot and mustardy*

Prep time: 10 minutes

Serves 2 to 3 *In this lovely salad, these bitter greens, beets, and radishes pair delightfully with nutty pumpkin seeds and a fruity vinaigrette. If you don't have pumpkin seeds, walnuts would be delicious also.*

FOR THE RASPBERRY VINAIGRETTE
⅓ cup extra-virgin olive oil
⅔ cup raspberry wine vinegar (if you don't have raspberry wine vinegar, use plain white wine vinegar)
1 tablespoon white sugar
2 teaspoons Dijon mustard
1 tablespoon raspberry jam
Salt
Freshly ground black pepper

FOR THE SALAD
1 large bunch watercress
2 beets, peeled and cut into matchsticks
3 radishes, thinly sliced
Toasted pumpkin seeds, for garnish

TO MAKE THE RASPBERRY VINAIGRETTE
In a small bowl, whisk together the olive oil, vinegar, sugar, mustard, and jam, and season with salt and pepper. (Or use a mason jar with a lid and shake it up.)

TO MAKE THE SALAD

Add the watercress to a bowl or to individual plates, and add the beets, radishes, and pumpkin seeds.

Drizzle the vinaigrette on top, and serve.

Prep time: 5 minutes | Cook time: 30 minutes

Serves 4 *This traditional French soup is velvety, simple, and delicious. Its green color makes you feel like you are eating spring. Swirl a little cream on top while serving for extra decoration.*

1 large bunch watercress, a few leaves reserved for garnish
2 large or 3 medium potatoes
3 tablespoons butter
1 onion, chopped
6 cups water
1 cup chicken stock or white wine
Salt
Freshly ground black pepper
½ cup heavy cream
2 egg yolks
Croutons, for garnish

Thoroughly wash the watercress.

Peel the potatoes and cut them into thin slices.

In a large pan over medium-high heat, melt the butter. Fry the onion and potatoes for about 5 minutes.

Add the watercress and stir for a few minutes, until wilted. Add the water and chicken stock or wine, and season with salt and pepper.

Turn down the heat and simmer for 30 minutes. Remove from the heat and cool slightly.

Transfer the mixture to a blender or food processor and purée until smooth.

In a small bowl, mix together the heavy cream with the egg yolks.

Return the puréed soup to the heat, and add the cream mixture. Heat until hot, but do not boil.

Serve garnished with watercress and croutons.

356

From the berbere spices of Ethiopia to the Cajun spices of Louisiana to za'atar of the Middle East, mixing your own blends is where things start getting exciting. By using distinctive combinations of most of the spices you already have in your kitchen, you can create dishes with flavors of Japan, China, Mexico, North Africa, India, France, and the Caucasus. Some of the blends might look intimidating to create yourself, but if you have what the French call *mise en place,* or *everything in place*—your food processor plugged in and a hot, dry skillet ready to roast some spices—you should have no problem making all of these blends at home.

Berbere

The traditional spice blend of berbere (pronounced "bare-BARE-ee") contains spices native to Ethiopia and Eritrea that are not always readily available in supermarkets. The traditional blend includes ajowan (a seed similar to oregano), nigella (similar to cumin seeds), korarima (a type of Ethiopian cardamom), and radhuni (similar to celery seed). However, you can still make a delicious blend without these spices (recipe follows). Ethiopian cuisine usually consists of a spicy *wat*, or stew, piled on top of a plate of sponge bread, called *injera*, and accompanied by a grain and vegetable or spinach dish. The injera is used to scoop up the food with the fingers. Ethiopia's mountainous terrain prevented its cuisines from being heavily influenced by other countries, but since it's along the route of the spice trade between Europe and Asia, it integrated these spices into its cuisines and continues to use them more than most other countries. It is said that the woman who can make the best berbere has the best chance of winning a good husband.

In the Kitchen *Berbere is actually a wonderful blend for those addicted to hot and pungent flavors. It can vary from mild to obscenely hot, though the amount of butter in a wat (also somewhat extreme by Western standards) tempers the blaze. Berbere is also fantastic as a rub for meat, poultry, and fish or as a seasoning for stews, soups, lentils, grains, spinach, and vegetables. It can be made dry or as a paste. Since roasting the hot peppers is an important component in creating the deep, dark, roasted flavor of the mix, while preparing the blend, you may need to hold your breath and periodically run to the door or window to take a breath of fresh air, and warn everyone in the house to stay outside.*

REGIONAL STAR
Ethiopia's national dish is *wott*, sometimes spelled *wat* or *wot*. Usually made with lamb, chicken, or beef, this spicy stew always contains the rich, deeply spicy berbere mix.

HEALING POWER
This mixture of spices contains properties that can increase circulation, relieve spasms and indigestion, help relieve arthritis, and help prevent cancer. It's also believed to be an aphrodisiac.

WHERE TO BUY IT: specialty grocery store, online, or make your own blend

HOW TO STORE IT: in an airtight container for a few months

COMPLEMENTS

---

chicken
lentils
spinach

PAIRS WELL WITH

garlic

FLAVOR PROFILE: *spicy, pungent, bitter, aromatic, rich*

Prep time: 30 minutes | Cook time: 3 hours

Serves 4 *Though this stew is fairly simple to make, the ingredients simmer on the stove in various stages for about 3 hours. The extreme amount of butter in this recipe helps temper the prodigious spice. You will need to keep the windows open while preparing this dish, but once they've tasted it, everyone will ask you to make it again and again.*

3 pounds chicken pieces, thighs or breasts, cut into bite-size pieces
1 lemon
1 teaspoon salt
1 pound butter
2 tablespoons minced fresh ginger, divided
2 teaspoons plus 2 tablespoons minced garlic, divided
1 teaspoon dried oregano
1 teaspoon fenugreek seeds
½ teaspoon ground allspice
½ teaspoon ground turmeric
½ teaspoon ground cardamom
2 tablespoons extra-virgin olive oil
3 cups finely minced yellow onions
¼ cup Berbere Spice Blend (here) or store bought
1 cup chicken stock
½ cup white or red wine
1 tablespoon tomato paste
4 hard-boiled eggs

In a glass bowl, squeeze the lemon over the chicken pieces and sprinkle them with the salt. Let them rest for 30 minutes.

In a small saucepan over medium heat, melt the butter.

Stir in 1 tablespoon of ginger, 2 teaspoons of garlic, the oregano, fenugreek seeds, allspice, turmeric, and cardamom. Reduce the heat to medium-low and simmer for about 30 minutes, until the milk solids remain at the bottom. Make sure the butter doesn't burn to avoid a bitter flavor. Reduce the heat if necessary.

Strain the foam off the top of the butter and pour the clear fat into a separate container, leaving the solids at the bottom of the pan (or strain through a cheesecloth).

In a large pot over medium heat, heat 2 tablespoons of spiced butter with the olive oil. Add the onions and sauté for 5 minutes.

Cover and cook over low heat for 25 minutes, stirring often.

Add another tablespoon of spiced butter, the remaining 2 tablespoons of garlic and 1 tablespoon of ginger, and continue to cook for an additional 15 minutes.

Add the Berbere Spice Blend and ⅓ cup of spiced butter, and sauté for an additional 10 minutes, stirring occasionally. Refrigerate any remaining spiced butter.

Add the chicken, stock, wine, and tomato paste, and increase the heat until the mixture begins to boil.

Reduce the heat to low and simmer, covered, for an additional 40 to 45 minutes, or until the chicken is tender.

The sauce should be thick. Continue to simmer without the lid if the sauce is too thin.

Taste and adjust the seasonings. Add more berbere for increased spiciness.

Add the boiled eggs and simmer for 10 to 15 more minutes.

Serve over rice or injera bread.

Prep time: 10 minutes | Cook time: 5 minutes

Makes about 1 cup *You can produce either a dry spice blend or a paste. If preparing a dry mixture, use only dried ingredients. For a paste, add ¼ cup of olive oil, water, or wine at the end. Some berbere spice blends include dried garlic, ginger, and onion powder. You can add a teaspoon of each, or for a richer flavor, add the fresh versions to the dish while you are preparing it.*

10 to 20 dried and seeded hot red chile peppers (depending on hot spice tolerance)
2 teaspoons coriander seeds
1 teaspoon fenugreek seeds
1 teaspoon cumin seeds
1 teaspoon black peppercorns
8 whole allspice berries or about 1 teaspoon ground allspice
Seeds of 5 cardamom pods
6 whole cloves
3 tablespoons ground paprika
½ teaspoon ground nutmeg
½ teaspoon ground cinnamon
½ teaspoon dried thyme (optional)

In a heavy, dry pan over high heat, dry roast the chiles for 2 to 3 minutes. Hold your breath when standing over them, and open all the windows.

Add the coriander seeds, fenugreek seeds, cumin seeds, peppercorns, allspice berries, cardamom seeds, and cloves, and roast for another 5 minutes, until all the spices darken slightly. Remove from the heat and cool.

In a spice grinder or using a mortar and pestle, grind the spice mixture.

Add the paprika, nutmeg, cinnamon, and thyme (if using), and mix well.

Store the dry spice blend in a dark, dry place.

Prep time: 5 minutes | Cook time: 20 minutes

Serves 2 *Red lentils have a nutty flavor and are smaller and quicker cooking than green or brown lentils. They become very soft with cooking, making them perfect for scooping up with Ethiopian injera bread or naan, but they are also great just eaten with a spoon. This rich, tomato-y stew enhanced with the heady spices of berbere makes a lovely light vegetarian entrée or a hearty and satisfying side dish.*

1 tablespoon olive oil
1 shallot, minced
1-inch piece fresh ginger, minced
3 garlic cloves, minced
2 tablespoons Berbere Spice Blend (here)
1 cup red lentils
1 (14-ounce) can diced, fire-roasted tomatoes, with juice
2 cups vegetable broth
½ teaspoon salt
¼ teaspoon pepper
¼ cup Greek yogurt, for garnish
2 tablespoons chopped cilantro, for garnish

Heat the oil in a medium saucepan set over medium heat. Add the shallot and ginger and cook, stirring, until softened, about 5 minutes. Stir in the garlic and the Berbere Spice Blend and stir to mix well.

Add the lentils and cook, stirring to coat, for about 1 minute more.

Add the tomatoes and their juice along with the vegetable broth. Bring to a boil, reduce the heat to low, cover, and simmer, stirring occasionally, for about 10 minutes, until the lentil are tender.

If the skillet becomes too dry before the lentils are cooked through, stir in a bit more water or broth.

Season with the salt and the pepper, and serve garnished with yogurt and cilantro.

Cajun Spice

While many countries have developed their spice mixtures over hundreds of years, North America has embraced the concept of celebrity spice blenders, especially regarding Cajun seasonings. Both Tony Chachere, considered to be the "Ol' Master" of Cajun cooking, and Chef Paul Prudhomme, who now has his own TV show, developed their own brand-name Cajun seasonings. These brands, as well as other commercial brands, tend to be considerably more salty and expensive than what you make at home. Some prepared Cajun blends contain only paprika, black pepper, cayenne, and a little onion powder. Even the "gourmet" ones only include other spices and herbs like celery seed, thyme, garlic, coriander, and cumin. The difference between Cajun and Creole seasonings is that Creole uses a bit more oregano. Cajun seasonings go into jambalayas, gumbos, and other foods spawned by the seaside in Louisiana, where you could throw crawdads, crabs, catfish, oysters, or even pieces of alligator all into a pot.

In the Kitchen *According to some Cajun chefs, white pepper, black pepper, paprika, and cayenne all touch different parts of the tongue, and they make up the base of Cajun seasonings. These spices pair well with the "holy trinity" that constitutes Cajun and Creole dishes: celery, bell peppers, and onions, cooked in a method borrowed from the French. Cajun cooking also inherited the French concept of the roux—butter mixed with flour to thicken a sauce or stew—though Louisiana chefs make it with bacon fat rather than butter. To make the roux for a gumbo, you stir the flour and fat together until it darkens, a process that can scent both your house and clothes. The darker the roux, the darker the meat you add to it. Cajun seasoning can be used as a rub for chicken or seafood or added to traditional jambalayas, gumbos, stews, sausages, beans, and rice.*

☀ REGIONAL STAR

Cajun and Creole cooking, as well as the 30 other regions in the world to where these seasonings are exported.

✚ HEALING POWER

Contains all the healing powers of the spices and herbs in the blend.

WHERE TO BUY IT: supermarket, online, or make your own blend

HOW TO STORE IT: in an airtight container for a few months

COMPLEMENTS

> **beans**
> **bell peppers**
> **black-eyed peas**
> **carrots**
> **celery**
> **gumbo**
> **jambalaya**

okra
onions
peas
rice
roux
sweet potatoes

bay leaf
cayenne pepper
cumin
garlic
oregano
paprika

FLAVOR PROFILE: *spicy, smoky, herbaceous*

Cajun Spice Blend

Prep time: 5 minutes

Makes ½ cup *Most Cajun seasonings contain onion and garlic powder. For a superior blend, omit those and add fresh garlic and onion directly to your dish. Or you can use 3 cloves of garlic and a chopped onion to make a paste that will last a week. You can rub the paste on meat to form a flavorful crust.*

- **1 tablespoon ground paprika**
- **1 teaspoon freshly ground black pepper**
- **½ teaspoon ground white pepper**
- **1 teaspoon ground cumin**
- **2 teaspoons ground cayenne pepper**
- **2 teaspoons dried thyme**
- **1 teaspoon dried sage**
- **1 teaspoon salt**
- **1 teaspoon anise or ground fennel seed**
- **½ teaspoon celery seed**
- **1 teaspoon mustard powder (optional)**

In a small bowl, stir together the paprika, black pepper, white pepper, cumin, cayenne pepper, thyme, sage, salt, anise, celery seed, and mustard powder (if using).

Store in an airtight container.

TIP: Many cooks claim that the only difference between Cajun and Creole seasoning is the addition of oregano and parsley. So for a Creole seasoning, add 1 teaspoon of each with a bay leaf.

Prep time: 10 minutes | Cook time: 30 minutes

Serves 6 *The word gumbo comes from the African word for okra, which was used as a thickener. The Choctaw Indians also taught Cajun cooks to use sassafras leaves as a thickener. In this recipe, thickening takes the simple form of a roux, but you don't have to stand over the pot, stirring it for 45 minutes—unless you want to, of course.*

½ pound andouille sausage, cut into ½-inch slices
2 tablespoons butter
5 tablespoons flour
1 cup chopped onion
1 cup chopped celery
4 garlic cloves, minced
1 bay leaf
1 medium green pepper, chopped
2 cups chicken broth
1 (28-ounce) can diced tomatoes
1 tablespoon Cajun Spice Blend (here), or store bought
4 cups chopped cooked chicken

In a large pan over high heat, cook the sausage for 5 minutes, stirring often.

Set the sausage aside on a paper towel–lined plate.

Add the butter to the fat from the sausage, and stir in the flour.

Whisk vigorously for 5 minutes over medium-high heat.

Add the onion, celery, garlic, bay leaf, and green pepper, and cook for 5 minutes.

Stir in the broth, tomatoes, and Cajun Spice Blend, and cook for 5 minutes.

Add the sausage and chicken, and simmer for 5 minutes to blend the spices.

Serve as a soup or over rice.

Curry Powder

. . . .

Garam Masala

Curry powder is actually a Western invention blended from the spices typically used in Indian curries. Most curry powders you purchase contain some combination of coriander, cumin, fenugreek, mustard seed, cayenne, black pepper, and turmeric. Others might include ginger, asafetida, fennel seed, cardamom, cinnamon, black pepper, and cloves. Sri Lankan and Madras curry powders have curry leaves in them and tend to be darker with more cardamom and cinnamon. The spice blend Indian chefs typically use is called garam masala, and it has as many blends as there are cooks in India. Garam masalas generally don't include turmeric, the spice that gives our version of curry powder its characteristic color. Some garam masalas emphasize clove and pepper in their blends, while others are heavier on the more aromatic spices like cinnamon, mace, nutmeg, cardamom, and sometimes even rose petals. Some garam masalas are better suited for meat and others for vegetables or lentils.

In the Kitchen *The curry powder blend you find in the supermarket is usually a simple mixture of turmeric, coriander, cumin, cayenne, and cinnamon, which you can add to eggs, chicken, tuna salad, or to any other dish that calls for basic curry powder. Use it on French fries, in mayonnaise or vinaigrette, or in pumpkin soup. An additional blend of garam masala is included here, in case you'd like to make more complex Indian food with other spices.* Garam masala *literally means* heat spice. *According to Ayurvedic teachings, however, heat should be monitored, as too much can light the body on fire. Indian chefs also use spices according to the season, believing, for example, that too much mace or nutmeg during the summer can cause a nosebleed. In order to become a good Indian chef, you must first become a good* masalchi, *one who has mastered the blending of spices. To achieve that, you must be comfortable with experimentation.*

❊ REGIONAL STAR
India and anywhere Indian curries are made.

✚ HEALING POWER
Contains all the digestive and antioxidant powers of all the participating spices.

WHERE TO BUY IT: supermarket, Asian or Indian market, or make your own

HOW TO STORE IT: airtight container

COMPLEMENTS

beef

carrots
cauliflower
coconut milk
eggplant
ghee
lamb
lentils
mushrooms
onions
peas
potatoes
poultry
rice
seafood
yogurt

PAIRS WELL WITH

cilantro
garlic
ginger

FLAVOR PROFILE: *spicy, sweet, pungent*

Whole Garam Masala (for rice)

Prep time: 5 minutes

Makes about ½ cup *Rather than grinding or blending, you can leave these spices whole and simply add them to rice while it's cooking to flavor the rice.*

6 green cardamom pods
6 cloves
2 cinnamon sticks
2 bay leaves
½ teaspoon ground mace

In a bowl, mix together the cardamom pods, cloves, cinnamon sticks, bay leaves, and mace.

Store in an airtight container.

Garam Masala Spice Blend

Prep time: 5 minutes

Makes about 1 cup *The specific spice blends of garam masalas pair with different types of meat in a similar way that people in the West pair wine with meat. This particular blend can be used for both white and dark meat curry dishes.*

1 tablespoon cumin seeds
1½ tablespoons cardamom seeds
2½ teaspoons black peppercorns
1 teaspoon coriander seeds
1 teaspoon fennel seeds
4 cinnamon sticks
1 teaspoon whole cloves
1 teaspoon mace
1 bay leaf
1 teaspoon ground ginger
½ teaspoon ground nutmeg

In a mortar and pestle or spice grinder, grind together the cumin seeds, cardamom seeds, peppercorns, coriander seeds, fennel seeds, cinnamon sticks, cloves, mace, bay leaf, ginger, and nutmeg.

Store in an airtight container.

Traditional Curry Powder Blend

Prep time: 5 minutes

Makes 1 cup *Use this traditional curry powder blend for recipes that call for curry powder. You can make a simpler variation by omitting the cloves and cardamom.*

4 tablespoons coriander seeds
3 tablespoons cumin seeds
½ tablespoon mustard seeds
2 tablespoons ground cinnamon
4 tablespoons black peppercorns
½ tablespoon ground cloves
1 tablespoon ground cardamom
1 tablespoon ground turmeric
1 tablespoon ground ginger
½ tablespoon cayenne pepper

In a mortar and pestle or spice grinder, grind together the coriander seeds, cumin seeds, mustard seeds, cinnamon, peppercorns, cloves, cardamom, turmeric, ginger, and cayenne pepper.

Store in an airtight container.

Easy Curry Chicken

Prep time: 30 minutes | Cook time: 45 minutes

Serves 4 *This is an easy but delicious chicken curry recipe that calls for curry powder. Most traditional Indian recipes scoff at the idea of curry powder, considering it to be an English invention. They prefer to call curry sauce a gravy made with a unique blend of spices. This Indian recipe, however, calls for curry powder, and it is simple and delicious.*

2 pounds boneless skinless chicken thighs
½ cup almonds
½ cup sesame seeds
2 tablespoons coconut oil, ghee, or other cooking oil
3 tablespoons Traditional Curry Powder Blend (here), or store bought
2 tablespoons peanut butter
1 (6-ounce) can tomato paste
Milk of 1 coconut or 1 (13-ounce) can coconut milk
Salt

Cut the chicken into bite-size pieces.

In a small pot of boiling water, blanch the almonds for 1 minute. Immediately strain them through a colander and rinse with cold water.

Remove the almond skins and cut the almonds in half.

In a small, dry pan over medium-high heat, roast the sesame seeds for 2 to 3 minutes, until golden brown.

In a food processor or blender, grind the almonds and sesame seeds together with a little water until the mixture becomes a paste.

In a large pan over medium-high heat, heat the oil.

Add the almond paste and fry for 1 minute.

Add the Traditional Curry Powder Blend, peanut butter, and tomato paste, and stir for an additional 1 to 2 minutes, until fragrant.

Add the coconut milk and salt, and turn down the heat to simmer for 20 minutes.

Add the chicken and cook for about 20 minutes, or until the chicken is tender. Add a little more water if the mixture becomes too thick.

Serve hot over rice.

Five-Spice Powder

Chinese five-spice blend, as opposed to the Indian five-spice blend called *panch phoron*, is a mixture of star anise, cloves, Chinese cinnamon (or cassia), fennel seeds, and Sichuan pepper. In other words, Chinese chefs were aiming for a superpower powder that blended all five flavors of spicy, salty, sweet, sour, and bitter. Depending on the region of origin, some recipes add orange peel, ginger root, white pepper, or galangal, as well. Sichuan pepper, also called Chinese coriander, is the only spice of the blend not profiled in this guide. It's related to neither black pepper nor chile pepper, and though it's usually possible to find in Asian markets, if you can't, simply substitute black pepper. Some recipes for the blend use the same proportions of each spice, and some highlight a specific one, star anise being the most common. The blend of these spices brings out the warm-sweet aspect of roasted vegetables and meat.

In the Kitchen *Chinese five-spice is found less often in traditional Chinese kitchens than in Chinese restaurants, where it's used in a process called "flavor potting," in which meat is cooked for many hours in a rich sauce made from the blend. Five-flower pork is one such dish. It's mostly used with fatty meats like pork and duck, since the spices actually help break down the fats during digestion. Dry roasting it with table salt can produce a seasoned salt for the table or a dry rub for a chicken. You can also mix it with raspberry jam and soy sauce as a marinade for chicken. For a quick vegetarian meal, mix it into Chinese noodles with garlic, ginger, and broccoli; or try it in an omelet, in braised tofu, on fruit salad, roasted carrots, sweet potatoes, steamed rice, or roasted peanuts, or even in chocolate fondue.*

❊ REGIONAL STAR
China and Chinese diaspora. Some restaurants in Hawaii use pure Chinese five-spice as a table condiment.

✚ HEALING POWER
Contains all the combined healing power of pepper, anise, cloves, cinnamon, and fennel; primarily, it's a digestive powerhouse.

WHERE TO BUY IT: supermarket, specialty grocery store, or blend your own for best flavor

HOW TO STORE IT: For best results, blend just before using.

COMPLEMENTS

braised meats
marinades
nuts
rice
roasted vegetables

tofu

garlic
ginger
turmeric

FLAVOR PROFILE: *spicy, sweet, bitter, pungent*

Chinese Five-Spice Blend

Prep time: 5 minutes

Makes about 4 tablespoons *Every chef varies their spice blend a little, either adding the same proportions of each spice or varying it. Most recipes are heavier on the star anise than any other spice and lighter on the cloves. As with all spice mixtures, they are better when some of the spices are dry roasted first and ground fresh.*

2 teaspoons Sichuan peppercorns
2 tablespoons fennel seeds
8 star anise seeds
2 teaspoons ground cinnamon
¼ teaspoon ground cloves

In a small pan over low heat, dry roast the pepper-corns until the aroma blooms, about 3 minutes.

Remove the peppercorns from the pan, and dry roast the fennel seeds.

Grind the peppercorns, fennel seeds, and star anise seeds in a spice or coffee grinder.

In a small bowl, mix in the cinnamon and cloves until you have a finely ground mixture.

For best results, use immediately.

TIP: If you can't find Sichuan pepper, you can substitute black pepper, as well as anise seed for star anise, but double the quantity of anise seed.

Roasted Chicken Breasts Marinated in Chinese Five-Spice Blend

Prep time: 10 minutes, plus 2 hours to marinate | Cook time: 45 minutes

Serves 2 *Because Chinese Five-Spice Blend complements ginger and garlic so well, you can't go wrong with this easy-to-make chicken dish. The flavors are dense enough to go beautifully with red wine.*

½ teaspoon salt
½ teaspoon freshly ground black pepper
2 tablespoons extra-virgin olive oil
2 teaspoons minced ginger
2 teaspoons minced garlic
2 teaspoons Chinese Five-Spice Blend (<u>here</u>), or store bought
2 whole chicken breasts, skin left on

In a small bowl, mix together the salt, pepper, olive oil, ginger, garlic, and Chinese Five-Spice Blend.

Place the chicken in a baking dish and slather it with the marinade.

Cover the chicken with aluminum foil and refrigerate it for at least 2 hours.

Preheat the oven to 350°F.

Bake the chicken, still covered with aluminum foil, for 45 minutes.

Serve alone or over rice.

Harissa

A Tunisian folktale states that a man can measure his wife's love by how spicy she prepares his food. If his food becomes bland, her love is waning. Harissa is as ubiquitous a condiment in North Africa as ketchup in North America, or maybe more so. Sold in cans, tubes, and even plastic bags along the road, harissa is served with almost every meal. A common breakfast in Tunisia consists of last night's bread dipped in spicy, garlicky harissa paste and olive oil. Each neighborhood has its own recipe, though dried red peppers, olive oil, garlic, and salt form the base mixture, and caraway, cumin, and coriander are usually added in varying proportions. Some cooks also add mint, sun-dried tomatoes, roasted bell pepper, carrots, preserved lemons, or rose petals. The flavors also depend on the type of red chiles used. Before red chiles arrived in Tunisia, black cumin was the base of this ancient condiment.

In the Kitchen *Use harissa as you might use sriracha, but since it's less sweet, it's even more versatile. Add it to a tuna sandwich on a long, crusty baguette with avocado. Since it's so spicy, drizzle it with olive oil to cut the heat. Dollop a spoonful alongside couscous with Moroccan Chicken (here), or add it to eggs. Harissa is added to a chickpea stew called* lablabi, *made with onion, garlic, cumin, and lemon and eaten for breakfast, and to* shakshuka, *a mixture of eggs and tomato sauce (the names alone make one hungry). Try adding harissa to spaghetti with sausage or to yogurt or mayonnaise for a dip. Add it to a honey vinaigrette to toss with a carrot and raisin salad. You can also stir it into hummus, top a pizza with it, or mix it into a marinade for fish or lamb. Adding it to the cooking water of rice or to couscous will impart a fragrant aroma and color.*

REGIONAL STAR
Tunisia, Algeria, Morocco

HEALING POWER
Contains all the immune-boosting powers of really spicy peppers and garlic.

WHERE TO BUY IT: in cans and tubes at Middle Eastern markets, in plastic bags on the streets of North Africa, online

HOW TO STORE IT: Keep homemade harissa in the refrigerator for a couple of weeks.

COMPLEMENTS

almonds
bread
capers
carrots
chickpea

couscous
dates
eggplant
eggs
figs
fish stew
goat
lamb
mayonnaise
olive oil
olives
potatoes
roasted red peppers
tagines
tomatoes
yogurt

PAIRS WELL WITH

caraway
chile pepper
cilantro
coriander
garlic
mint
parsley
saffron

FLAVOR PROFILE: *spicy with caraway and cumin notes*

Prep time: 45 minutes | Cook time: 2 minutes

Makes about 2 cups *You can find a variety of dried red peppers in an Asian, Middle Eastern, or Mexican market or in the international section of the supermarket. Best to use a blender or food processor, as it's hard to macerate peppers in a mortar and pestle. Try using guajillo chiles or New Mexican. It's worth making a large quantity of this since it will last a month in the refrigerator, and in a little jar, it makes a great gift, too.*

25 to 30 dried red chile peppers
1½ teaspoons cumin seed
1½ teaspoons coriander seed
1 teaspoon caraway seed
1½ teaspoons salt
10 garlic cloves
1 tablespoon freshly squeezed lemon juice
1 to 1½ cups extra-virgin olive oil

Remove the stems and seeds from the dried red peppers. When you remove the stem from the pepper, turn it upside down and shake it. The seeds should fall out easily. It's easier to remove the seeds when the peppers are dry than after you've soaked them.

Soak the peppers in a glass bowl of warm water covered with a plate for 30 minutes.

While the peppers are soaking, in a small, dry pan over high heat, toast the cumin seed, coriander seed, and caraway seed, swirling them around until they darken slightly, about 2 minutes.

Empty the spices onto a plate and cool.

In a food processor or blender, pulse the soaked peppers, toasted spices, salt, and garlic until the mixture reaches a smooth consistency. (You will still see tiny chunks of red pepper.)

Slowly add the lemon juice and olive oil, pulsing until well blended. Taste (a tiny bit), and add more salt if needed.

Store the harissa, topped with a little olive oil, in a glass jar in the refrigerator.

Prep time: 5 minutes | Cook time: 10 minutes

Serves 3 to 4 *These spicy, flavorful eggs can also be eaten for dinner. Serve with bread to sop up the sauce and extra harissa on the side for the hotties in your life.*

1 onion, chopped
3 tablespoons extra-virgin olive oil, divided
2 garlic cloves, minced
2 heaping tablespoons tomato paste
2 heaping tablespoons Harissa Paste (<u>here</u>), or store bought
½ cup water
6 eggs, divided
Avocado slices, for garnish (optional)
Cilantro, for garnish (optional)

In a medium frying pan over medium-high heat, sauté the onion with 2 tablespoons of olive oil until soft and slightly golden, about 6 minutes.

Add the garlic and sauté for 30 seconds.

Add the remaining 1 tablespoon of oil to the pan, and lightly fry the tomato paste in it by stirring it around (this process sweetens the tomato paste) for about a minute.

Add the Harissa Paste and enough water to make a sauce that is neither thick nor runny.

Add 3 eggs, and stir them around into the mix so that the yolks are broken.

Add the remaining 3 eggs, but keep those yolks whole.

Carefully cover the eggs with the tomato sauce to help them cook until the yolks are cooked but slightly runny, about 3 minutes.

Top with the slices of avocado and the cilantro (if using), and serve.

Herbes de Provence

French cooking has developed a whole array of savory herbal blends. A bouquet garni, or *herb bundle* in French, is a bundle of herbs tied together by their stems and added to stocks. They are usually hearty herbs, which can withstand slow cooking, and include a mixture of basil, bay leaf, peppercorns, parsley, savory, rosemary, sage, and tarragon, depending on which type of meat was used to make the stock. *Fines herbes* are the more delicate herbs added at the end of cooking and include tarragon, chervil, parsley, and chives, but herbes de Provence is the most common blend you will find in the spice rack of your local supermarket. A blend of dried herbs growing in the Provence region of the South of France, it typically contains rosemary, savory, sage, thyme, marjoram, and oregano. Sometimes lavender is added to a blend for the American market, though lavender is not traditionally used in French cooking.

In the Kitchen *Unlike the more delicate* fines herbes, *herbes de Provence are added at the beginning of cooking or sautéed in the oil that will be used in cooking. Add this blend to any food you want to taste more "French." It's most commonly used to make rubs for grilled meats and baked chicken, but you can also substitute it for the salt shaker on your table as a healthy alternative to salt. Add it to trout with lemon or to sautéed mushrooms, boiled potatoes, or asparagus. It's probably most suited as a rub for a chicken roasting in the oven surrounded by carrots and potatoes, but it also goes well with lamb simmered in a red wine sauce. The recipe for the blend as follows uses dried herbs, but you can always use fresh when available. According to preference, some French chefs also add basil, bay leaves, fennel seeds, and sage to their blends.*

REGIONAL STAR
France and anywhere else in the world that practices French cooking.

HEALING POWER
Contains all the healing powers of all the blended herbs, though drying them weakens their medicinal strength.

WHERE TO BUY IT: supermarket, specialty grocery store, online, or blend your own

HOW TO STORE IT: in an airtight container for up to several months

COMPLEMENTS

asparagus
butter
carrots
chicken
fish

lamb
mushrooms
olive oil
potatoes
rice
tomatoes

PAIRS WELL WITH

---

basil
bay leaf
fennel
parsley
pepper
sage
salt
tarragon

FLAVOR PROFILE: *thyme, marjoram, oregano, savory, rosemary, and lavender notes*

Prep time: 5 minutes

Makes ½ cup *This recipe offers the option to include lavender or leave it out, as it is often used in the North American versions of the blend.*

3 tablespoons dried thyme
1 tablespoon dried marjoram
1 tablespoon dried oregano (can substitute extra marjoram for the oregano and vice versa)
1 tablespoon dried savory
2 teaspoons dried rosemary
1 teaspoon dried lavender (optional)

In a small bowl, stir together the thyme, marjoram, oregano, savory, rosemary, and lavender (if using).

Store in an airtight container.

Prep time: 15 minutes | Cook time: 1 hour to 1 hour, 30 minutes

Serves 4 to 6 *Herbes de Provence is a particularly suitable spice mixture to sprinkle over a roasting chicken. It also goes with the potatoes and root vegetables you've baked along with it.*

¼ cup extra-virgin olive oil
1 whole 2- to 3-lb chicken
Salt
Freshly ground black pepper
¼ cup Herbes de Provence Blend (here), or store bought
2 potatoes, peeled and cut into ¾-inch cubes
2 carrots, cut into 1-inch logs
1 onion, peeled and cut into chunks
8 whole garlic cloves, skin removed
1 lemon, sliced

Preheat the oven to 450°F.

On a plate, rub the olive oil over the chicken, season it with the salt and pepper, and sprinkle on the Herbes de Provence Blend.

On a large baking sheet, roast the chicken, potatoes, carrots, onions, and garlic for about 30 minutes, until the chicken begins to brown.

Reduce the heat to 350°F and bake until done, about 30 minutes to an hour more.

Serve garnished with the lemon slices.

Khmeli Suneli

Khmeli suneli in the Georgian language literally means *dried spices*, and every region (and practically every family) in the republic of Georgia has its own variation. Traditionally, *khmeli suneli*, also known as "housewife spices," contains mixtures of coriander, fenugreek leaves, fenugreek seeds, ground marigold, mint, dill, summer savory, fennel seeds, cinnamon, cloves, pepper, bay leaf, basil, thyme, saffron, parsley, celery seed, safflower, hot pepper, and sumac. This blend creates a deep, earthy, grassy, bitter flavor, complementing the Persian, Russian, and Turkish conglomeration that makes up Georgian food, though Georgians would just say their food is simply "of the earth." To make this spice blend properly, you should know the spice vendor and the slope upon which his spices are grown, and you should probably be on good terms with his cow as well. Fresh meats, cheeses, yogurts, and vegetables all pair well with the *khmeli suneli* spices and the copious amounts of garlic, cilantro, walnuts, and pomegranates added to them.

In the Kitchen *Georgian cooks add* khmeli suneli *to slightly under-ripe plums in the spring, boiled with garlic, dill, cilantro, and salt to make a sour but pungent sauce called* tkemali *for spooning over grilled meat. You can add it to chicken with garlic-walnut sauce, or make a marinade with* khmeli suneli *and wine for kebabs. Try it in a mayonnaise with cilantro and garlic on fried eggplant, in Georgian Eggplant (here), or in the ground walnut-spinach salad called* phkali. *Add it to pinto beans with onions for a satisfying side dish called* lobio. *These spices are also used to flavor stews containing beef and nightshades. You can even add them to eggs. For maximum flavor, try growing some of the herbs in this mix yourself.*

REGIONAL STAR
Essential to the cuisine of the republic of Georgia and the countries of the Caucasus region.

HEALING POWER
Whether it's this spice mixture, the mountain air, or the amount of garlic Georgians eat, they live longer than anyone else in the world.

WHERE TO BUY IT: specialty grocery store, online, or blend your own. You might need to go to a specialty grocery store or look online to find some of the ingredients, like ground fenugreek seeds and marigold.

HOW TO STORE IT: in an airtight container for a few months, though Georgians would never dream of keeping it that long

COMPLEMENTS

beef
bell peppers
chicken
eggplant

**eggs
fish
lamb
nettles
plums
potatoes
soups
spinach
tomatoes
walnuts
yogurt**

PAIRS WELL WITH

**basil
cilantro
garlic
parsley**

FLAVOR PROFILE: *warm, earthy, bitter, nutty, grassy*

Prep time: 5 minutes

Makes about 1 cup *According to legend, a tea made from this mix was used to restore an exhausted army in the twelfth century. Every family in the republic of Georgia has its own* khmeli suneli *spice blend. This is the deluxe version.*

2 tablespoons dried marjoram (or oregano)
2 tablespoons dried dill weed
2 tablespoons dried mint
2 tablespoons dried parsley
2 tablespoons dried summer savory
2 tablespoons coriander seeds
2 tablespoons ground fenugreek seeds
2 tablespoons dried marigold powder (omit if you can't find it)
1 tablespoon freshly ground black pepper
2 bay leaves, crushed
1 teaspoon dried basil
1 teaspoon dried thyme
Pinch saffron (optional)
½ teaspoon fennel seeds (optional)

In a small bowl, stir together the marjoram, dill weed, mint, parsley, summer savory, coriander seeds, fenugreek seeds, marigold powder, black pepper, bay leaves, basil, thyme, saffron (if using), and fennel (if using).

Store in an airtight container.

Satsivi, or Chicken with Walnuts

This recipe by Christina Nichol originally appeared in *Lucky Peach*.

- -

Prep time: 1 hour | Cook time: 1 hour

Serves 4 Satsivi *is holiday food, especially when made with turkey. It tastes like warm earth—if the earth were that delicious. This key to this dish is the walnuts. They must be "not too sweet and not too bitter." You will need a long afternoon to make this, preferably with a sister or someone who feels like one, because the texture of the walnuts has to be right in order for this dish to work, and grinding them properly can be a somewhat arduous process.*

**1 whole chicken (or small turkey)
2½ cups walnuts
1 onion, chopped
2 tablespoons *Khmeli Suneli* Spice Blend (here), or store bought
1 bunch fresh cilantro, thoroughly washed
3 to 4 garlic cloves
1 tablespoon white wine vinegar
Salt**

In a large pot filled with enough water to cover the chicken over high heat, boil the chicken with the chopped onion until it is tender, about 60 minutes. Reserve the broth.

While the chicken is cooking, in a mortar (preferably one made from the boxwood tree that grows in Abkhazia and that's been in the family for six generations), pound the walnuts. The walnuts cannot be ground too fine and also must not have any pebble-size pieces in them. (This is the part where you have to sit and painstakingly pick out any larger pieces.)

Transfer the walnuts to a large bowl and add the onion, *Khmeli Suneli* Spice Blend, cilantro, garlic, vinegar, and a little of the reserved chicken broth.

Squeeze the mixture with your hands just until the oil begins to separate. Add more broth until the sauce lightens a little in color and has the texture of watery hummus.

When the chicken has cooled, remove the meat from the bone, leaving a few pieces whole. Add the chicken to the bowl, coat and mix with the walnut sauce, and season with salt.

Serve at room temperature.

Mole Poblano

In Mexican cuisine, the word *mole* refers to any sauce, which helps explain the word *guacamole*. Recently, mole has come to refer to one of the chile-based red, green, black, or yellow sauces famous in different regions of Mexico, especially in the states of Puebla and Oaxaca. Mole poblano, from Puebla, is considered Mexico's national dish. Theories about its origin vary. Some say nuns from the Convent of Santa Rosa in Puebla had to quickly make a sauce for the archbishop, so they threw together some dried bread, nuts, chili powder, spices, and chocolate, and poured it over a turkey. Oaxaca, known as the "land of the seven moles," makes a mole negro, which also contains chocolate and over 30 ingredients, some of which can only be found in Oaxaca's mountainous terrain. In the mountains south of Mexico City, some communities are sustained by mole-making cooperatives. They make a signature mole with almonds, producing over 30,000 tons a year for Mexican consumption, though mole is still relatively unknown in North America.

In the Kitchen *Mole poblano is traditionally served over turkey but can also be poured over chicken, pork, rice, tamales, enchiladas, or even poached eggs and toast for a Mexican version of eggs Benedict. Ingredients are roasted and ground into a powder or paste, which traditionally took a day or more but is considerably easier now with blenders and food processors. It's still labor-intensive, however, since the thickness of the sauce comes from reducing it over heat and stirring continuously for a long time. You can buy mole paste at Mexican markets or online, but nothing can really rival homemade mole. The rich flavor comes from combining at least two types of chile peppers, including ancho, chipotle, pasilla, and mulato, plus adding some of the following: tomatoes, tomatillos, garlic, sesame seeds, dried fruit, pumpkin seeds, cinnamon, cloves, anise, peanuts, pine nuts, and sometimes even tortillas, grapes, and plantains.*

REGIONAL STAR
Mexico, North America, Europe

HEALING POWER
Contains all the medicinal and antioxidant healing properties of chile peppers and the spices in this blend.

WHERE TO BUY IT: buy the paste at a Mexican market or online

HOW TO STORE IT: The homemade paste will keep for a few days in the refrigerator. It also freezes well. The packaged paste will keep for up to six months and can also be frozen.

COMPLEMENTS

chicken
chile peppers
chocolate

eggs
onion
plantains
pork
sour cream
tomatillos
tomato
tortillas
turkey

PAIRS WELL WITH

---

anise
cilantro
cinnamon
cloves
garlic
pepper

FLAVOR PROFILE: *nutty, deep-roasted flavor with sweet and spicy notes*

Prep time: 15 minutes | Cook time: 1 hour, 20 minutes

Makes 2 cups *This insanely delicious mole contains a mixture of four different chile peppers, nuts, spices, and chocolate. Use Mexican chocolate if you can find it; otherwise, use dark chocolate. If you only use two kinds of dried chiles, use anchos and mulatos.*

½ cup cooking oil
6 dried ancho chiles, stemmed and seeded
6 dried pasilla chiles, stemmed and seeded
3 dried mulato chiles, stemmed and seeded
2 dried chipotle chiles, stemmed and seeded
¼ cup almonds
¼ cup sesame seeds
¼ cup pumpkin seeds
¼ cup raisins
1 onion, chopped
6 garlic cloves
1 teaspoon anise seeds
1 teaspoon cumin seeds
1 teaspoon black peppercorns
4 whole cloves
1 cinnamon stick
⅓ cup Mexican or dark chocolate
1 tablespoon sugar
2 charred tomatoes
3 corn tortillas, ripped into small pieces
3½ cups chicken broth
Salt
Freshly ground black pepper

In a large pan over medium-high heat, heat the oil. Deep-fry the ancho, pasilla, mulato, and chipotle peppers, stirring often, until slightly darkened, about 3 minutes. Remove from the oil and set aside.

Add the almonds, sesame seeds, and pumpkin seeds to the pan and stir for about 3 minutes, until lightly toasted.

Add the raisins to the pan and roast until they are plump, about 3 minutes, and set aside.

Sauté the onion in the same pan for about 10 minutes, until golden, adding the garlic during the last 2 minutes and more oil if necessary.

In a large, dry pan over high heat, swirl the anise seeds, cumin seeds, peppercorns, cloves, and cinnamon, roasting for about 2 minutes, until fragrant.

In a large saucepan, mix all the roasted and sautéed ingredients together. Add the chili paste, chocolate, sugar, tomatoes, corn tortillas, and chicken broth. Cook over low heat for an hour, stirring often.

Add the whole mixture to a food processor and purée until smooth.

Season with salt and pepper and serve over grilled or poached chicken, or keep in the refrigerator for a few days. If the sauce is too thick, thin with water or broth.

TIP: Ancho peppers are the name for dried poblano peppers, otherwise known as "wide peppers," and in their fresh form, they are the peppers used to make chile rellenos. Mulatos are similar to anchos but darker in color and sweeter in flavor. Chipotle peppers are actually jalapeño peppers that have been smoked and dried.

Pasilla chiles are long, dark-skinned peppers with a licorice-prune flavor and are quite spicy.

Easy Chicken Mole Enchiladas

Prep time: 10 minutes | Cook time: 10 minutes

Serves 2 (Makes 6 enchiladas) *Since you've already done all the hard work making the mole paste, preparing these enchiladas is the easy part. The recipe doubles well for if you're serving four or want leftovers—which you probably will.*

> **1 cup shredded, cooked chicken**
> **1 cup Mole Poblano (<u>here</u>), divided**
> **6 corn tortillas**
> **¼ cup sour cream**
> **½ cup crumbled queso fresco (soft, un-aged white cheese)**
> **¼ bunch fresh cilantro leaves, chopped**

In a saucepan over medium heat, mix the shredded chicken with ½ cup of mole sauce, until bubbling.

In a separate saucepan over medium heat, heat the remaining ½ cup of mole sauce until bubbling.

While the mixture is heating, in a skillet over medium heat, toast the tortillas until soft.

Fill each tortilla with one-sixth of the chicken mixture, roll each tortilla up, and put 3 tortillas, seam-side down, on each warm plate.

Cover the enchiladas with the additional mole sauce, sour cream, queso fresco, and cilantro, and serve immediately.

**Prep time: 5 minutes, plus 30 minutes to marinate |
Cook time: 10 minutes**

Serves 2 *Mole poblano is commonly served over poultry or
enchiladas, but the rich sauce is a great counterpoint to delicate
prawns. Serve with warm corn tortillas for scooping up the prawns
and sauce.*

**1 pound peeled and deveined prawns
2 tablespoons extra-virgin olive oil, divided
Zest and juice of one lemon, divided
4 garlic cloves, thinly sliced
½ teaspoon salt
¼ teaspoon freshly ground black pepper
1 cup Mole Poblano (here)
2 tablespoons chopped cilantro**

In a medium bowl, toss the prawns with 1 tablespoon olive oil, lemon
zest, garlic, salt, and pepper. Cover and refrigerate for 30 minutes.

Place the mole sauce in a large skillet and bring to a simmer over
medium heat. Keep warm over low heat. If the sauce is too thick,
add a bit of water or broth to thin it.

In another large skillet, heat the remaining tablespoon of olive oil
over medium-high heat. Remove the prawns from the marinade,
reserving the marinade, and add them to the skillet in a single layer
(you may need to cook the prawns in batches).

Sear each prawn on one side, about 2 minutes, until lightly browned,
and then transfer it to the skillet with the mole sauce in it. Continue

cooking the prawns in the simmering sauce until they are cooked through, about 3 minutes more.

Once all of the prawns have been transferred to the mole sauce, deglaze the prawn skillet pan with the lemon juice, scraping up any browned bits from the bottom of the pan. Stir in the reserved marinade and pour the liquid from the skillet into the mole sauce and prawns.

Stir in the cilantro and serve immediately.

Seven-Spice Powder

Shichimi Togarashi

Togarashi means *spice* in Japanese, but like wasabi, the heat is meant to complement the other flavors of the food rather than dominate them. This blend of seven spices goes back to seventeenth-century Japan. While most of the spice blends in this guide are distinctive mixtures of the spices and herbs you recognize, Japanese seven-spice contains flavors not yet encountered but which are fairly easy to acquire, especially at an Asian market and probably at most local supermarkets. Orange peel and dried seaweed are the dominating aromas, while the pepper flakes and sansho, or Sichuan pepper, give it a slightly numbing tang. The sesame seeds and ginger round out its characteristic "Japanese flavor." You can adjust the seasonings to make it hot or mild by the proportion of hot chili flakes you add. Substitute dried orange peel for tangerine peel, or cayenne pepper for the pepper flakes, and poppy seeds for the traditional hemp seeds.

In the Kitchen *Japanese seven-spice makes a good condiment for buckwheat or soba noodles to give them a distinctive Japanese flavor. Use it at the table instead of salt, and sprinkle it over steamed rice or a baked potato for a quick and interesting snack. Sprinkle it on teriyaki chicken or anything you want to taste "Japanese," like rice cakes or crackers. This seasoning pairs well with other Japanese flavorings like sesame oil, soy sauce, and rice vinegar, giving food a pleasing oceanic flavor. It can go into broths, or even on top of sushi. It goes especially well with oily fish like eel or foods like tempura. Zest up steamed carrots or other root vegetables with a sprinkling of this spice, or add it to marinades or a dipping sauce for fish. To make a marinade for yakitori, mix together ¼ cup each of soy sauce, mirin, and sake, plus 1 tablespoon sugar. Marinate the chicken, grill, and sprinkle Japanese seven-spice on top.*

✳ REGIONAL STAR
Japan

✛ HEALING POWER
Contains all the healing powers of pepper and sesame as well as the potassium found in seaweed.

WHERE TO BUY IT: specialty grocery store, online, or make your own

HOW TO STORE IT: in an airtight container for a few weeks

COMPLEMENTS

chicken
crackers
mirin

noodles
pickles
potatoes
rice
rice wine vinegar
sake
sesame oil
soy sauce

PAIRS WELL WITH

---

cilantro
garlic
ginger
green onion
parsley

FLAVOR PROFILE: *spicy, citrusy, with notes of the ocean*

Prep time: 5 minutes | Cook time: 30 minutes to dry citrus peel

Makes 1 cup *Find flaked nori for this spice blend at Asian markets, or buy nori for making sushi and crush it. You can find sansho, the unripened pods of the Japanese prickly ash, at specialty grocery stores. They have a sharp, citrusy taste that can linger on the tongue up to ten minutes after tasting them. Black pepper or Chinese Sichuan pepper can be substituted for sansho.*

2 tablespoons whole red chiles
4 tablespoons sancho or 2 tablespoons black peppercorns
2 tablespoons dried tangerine peel or orange peel
1 teaspoon grated lime peel (optional)
1 tablespoon dried ginger
1½ tablespoons black sesame seeds
1 teaspoon poppy seeds (optional)
2 tablespoons flaked nori
1½ tablespoons hemp seeds (optional)

Using a mortar and pestle or food processor, grind the red chiles with the sancho.

Add the tangerine peel, lime peel (if using), ginger, and sesame seeds, and pulse gently. Do not grind to a paste or powder.

Place in a small bowl and stir together with the poppy seeds (if using), flaked nori, and hemp seeds (if using).

Put the mixture in a salt shaker or small bowl for garnishing Asian or Japanese dishes.

TIP: In order to make dried citrus peel, preheat the oven to 150° and bake fresh orange, tangerine, lemon, or lime peel on a baking sheet for 45 minutes or until the peels have thinned out and shrunk. Cool and pound in a mortar and pestle or in a food processor.

Simple Japanese One-Bowl Breakfast

Prep time: 5 minutes | Cook time: 5 minutes

Serves 2 *A traditional Japanese breakfast consists of rice, a bowl of miso soup, pickles, and a specially prepared omelet. This is a simple one-bowl variation that you can also eat for lunch, using the leftovers you have in the refrigerator.*

1 tablespoon sesame oil or other cooking oil
2 tablespoons chopped green onion
2 tablespoons soy sauce
2 cups cooked rice
½ to 1 cup leftover cooked vegetables like broccoli or carrots
½ to 1 cup leftover meat or fish
2 eggs
1 teaspoon rice wine vinegar
Japanese Seven-Spice Powder (here), or store bought

In a medium frying pan over medium heat, heat the oil. Sauté the green onion with the soy sauce for about a minute.

Add the rice and any leftover vegetables and meat or fish, and sauté until hot, about 2 minutes.

Stir the eggs and rice wine vinegar into the rice mixture and cook until the eggs are just barely cooked, about 2 minutes.

Sprinkle as much Japanese Seven-Spice Powder on top as desired, and serve hot.

TIP: To make your own teriyaki sauce, stir together soy sauce, fresh ginger, fresh garlic, rice wine vinegar, brown sugar, and honey in a saucepan over low heat until combined.

Za'atar

In the Middle East, za'atar is as common as ketchup in North America, but for centuries, every family closely guarded its own za'atar secret blend, sometimes even keeping it from their daughters. More a blend of herbs than spices, the mixture, depending on the region, contains a base of oregano and thyme (from which its name derives), plus, according to the region, a blend of additional spices that include marjoram, black pepper, cumin, coriander, fennel seeds, mint, parsley, sage, sesame seeds, salt, savory, sumac, dill, and dried orange peel. The herbs are traditionally dried in the sun and then coarsely ground with salt, sesame seeds, and any other spices. It has a pleasant crunch and fragrant, lemony aroma. Each region where it's used—Egypt, Iraq, Israel, Jordan, Palestine, Morocco, Saudi Arabia, Turkey, and Armenia—has their own variations. Palestinian versions include caraway seeds, while Lebanese versions are heavy on the sumac.

In the Kitchen *Arab bakers traditionally mix za'atar into olive oil and bake it into bread to give it a warm, earthy flavor. In Middle Eastern households, pita bread dipped in olive oil and then dipped in za'atar makes a popular breakfast or snack, especially before a test, as it's believed to be good for the brain. It makes a wonderful rub for grilled chicken and vegetables, as well as a topping for hummus or mixed into yogurt with chopped onions, lemon, and olive oil. Eat it on popcorn or even out of the jar on its own. It can be substituted for lemon juice on fish or sprinkled over a tomato-cucumber salad. You can also season your own flatbread with it using pizza dough.*

REGIONAL STAR

North Africa and the Middle East use this spice mixture in hummus, eggplant, and yogurt dips; on kebabs and lamb chops; to flavor falafel; in lentils, olives, eggs, and chickpea dishes; and as a topping for breads. In Oman, a tea is brewed with boiled water and za'atar.

HEALING POWER

It is a blend of the powerful antioxidant properties of all the combined dried spices and herbs that make up the mix. The fresher it is, the more powerful.

WHERE TO BUY IT: Middle Eastern market, or make it at home

HOW TO STORE IT: in a jar in a dark, dry place

COMPLEMENTS

cauliflower
chickpeas
cucumbers
dips
eggplant
eggs

falafel
feta
garlic
grilled vegetables and meat
hummus
lentils
olive oil
olives
pine nuts
pistachio
potatoes
yogurt

PAIRS WELL WITH

fennel
rosemary
saffron

FLAVOR PROFILE: *sour and nutty with notes of marjoram, thyme, and sesame*

Za'atar Spice Blend

Prep time: 5 minutes

Makes 1 cup *Traditionally these fresh herbs are dried together out in the sun. You can do that as well, or use dried herbs (the more recently dried, the better).*

1 teaspoon sea salt
3 tablespoons dried oregano
1 tablespoon dried marjoram
2 tablespoons roasted sesame seeds
2 tablespoons dried thyme
1 teaspoon ground cumin
1 teaspoon ground coriander
¼ cup sumac
1 teaspoon dried mint
1 teaspoon dried summer savory
1 tablespoon ground lemon or orange peel (optional)

In a food processor, pulse the salt, oregano, marjoram, sesame seeds, thyme, cumin, coriander, sumac, mint, summer savory, and lemon peel (if using) until a course meal is produced.

Store in a plastic bag or mason jar in a dark, dry place for up to 6 months.

TIP: Experiment with your own proportions of spices and herbs, and create your own closely guarded za'atar family blend.

Dave's Kitchen Sink Dry-Rub Chicken

Prep time: 5 minutes | Cook time: 1 hour to 1 hour, 30 minutes

Serves 4 *Sociale restaurant owner David Nichol uses this rub at least once a week when he grills chicken at home. Colonel Sanders put 11 secret spices and herbs in his original fried chicken recipe—this rub contains more, and doesn't have the monosodium glutamate. David says the most important ingredient is za'atar. He keeps a huge jar of it in his spice cupboard.*

Extra-virgin olive oil
1½ tablespoons maple syrup
1 whole chicken
Salt
Freshly ground black pepper
1½ teaspoons paprika
1½ teaspoons Za'atar Spice Blend (<u>here</u>), or store bought
½ teaspoon chili powder or cayenne pepper (optional)
1 lemon, halved

Preheat the oven to 350°F.

On a plate, rub the olive oil and maple syrup over the chicken. Season with salt and pepper.

Spread the paprika, Za'atar Spice Blend, chili powder, and pretty much anything else you have in your spice cupboard over the chicken if you need more spice to thoroughly coat the chicken.

Bake for 60 to 90 minutes, until the chicken is done and tender when cut into.

Squeeze a fresh lemon over the chicken, carve, and serve.

TIP: Ayurvedic medicine is based on the principle that the digestive tract is like a fire in the furnace. Too hot and it will burn out your energy; too cold and you will lose the fire. You, as the fire-keeper, need to keep the fire going without letting it get too hot and causing heartburn or other digestive disorders, or too cold and causing sluggishness. Certain foods are warming foods, and others are cooling. You eat foods according to your body type, your disposition, and the weather. The hot season can cause rashes, skin irritation, and even heat stroke. Ayurvedic cooling spices and herbs include mint, fennel, cilantro, coriander, cardamom, saffron, dill, and cumin —many of the spices and herbs found in za'atar.

Printed in Great Britain
by Amazon

14784229R00251